Scott Grates' words of wisdom ring true. Relationships matter and doing good is doing right by others. *Referrals Done Right* is a practical book with simple strategies that any small business owner can use to achieve long-term sustainability and growth. Scott shares what he and I agree matters most—That at the end of the day it really is all about the circle of grace.

DAVID CASULLO
Author, Entrepreneur, Up builder

In this book, Scott shares his history, struggles, determination and successes, and parses them out in a way that meets the reader where they are, and can be implemented in a variety of fields and experiences. Scott eschews traditional selling models in favor of a relationship-based approach to his business and gives the reader a step-by-step path to their own successes.

ANN RUSHLO
REALTOR® Association Executive/Leadership Consultant

Referrals Done Right is honest, straightforward and ingeniously witty. Exactly how Scott approaches life and what has made him a successful and respected small business owner and human. His strategies aren't just insightful in theory, they are practical and proven in the real world.

CARRIE MCMURRAY
Vice President Paige Marketing Communications Group

If you want your business to be successful, then *Referrals Done Right* is a must-read. I believe *Referrals Done Right* can be a valuable resource to help guide businesses to achieve profitability and success.

RAYMOND J. DURSO, JR.
President & CEO of The Genesis Group

Referrals Done Right is a must-read for anyone looking to expand their network and grow their business in a meaningful way. Scott presents an outline with practical, easy-to-implement strategies that transform the art of referrals into tangible results for small business owners.

CHRISTOPHER C. GIAMBRONE, CFP®, AIF®
Cofounder of CG Capital, Financial Life Management

Referrals done right is one of the first books you should read when opening a business. And if you're already in business, drop everything and read it ASAP. These actionable concepts put you in the driver's seat cruising towards higher productivity while controlling your marketing budget and lifting those around you. A true win, win, win!

KIRA SCHNELL-HARRISON
Insurance Agency Owner and Sales Trainer

This is a book I wish I had read 13 years ago when I started my business. The best and healthiest business is a referral from a happy client; that's something I had to learn the hard way. Excellent book for anyone looking to learn more about the power of serving their community, multiplying introductions and increasing retention.

HAYK TADEVOSYAN
entrepreneur, speaker, author of "The Power of Mindset."

Scott Grates didn't just write a book about referrals. He created an empowering resource for small business owners and their teams to take action with. Referrals can make or break your business, and *Referrals Done Right* takes away all of your excuses. You have the choice to become massively successful, or not.

ALEX SHATTUCK
CEO Auto Pilot Recruiting, Best Selling Author of Small Business BIG Recruiting, owner of multiple nationally-recognized insurance agencies.

Here is a great book—In these pages Scott shares valuable gems on how to win in business. The lessons learned from his own battles with the Goliath's in the Industry provide lessons learned for all of us. People love to do business with those they "like and trust" and Scott does an excellent job helping you know how to make that happen.

RANDY THOMPSON
author of "Paychecks Never Lie" and "Bigger Paychecks, Better Paychecks"

The Infinite Referral Advantage is an absolute must for every small business owner. Scott hits the nail on the head with his straightforward down to earth approach as he offers practical and actionable steps to ensuring you are on the right path to a lifetime of referrals and success. I couldn't put this book down once I started it and I kept thinking my only regret was to not find this book 10 years earlier in my career.

BRENT HERSHEY
Insurance Agency Owner

REFERRALS
DONE RIGHT

**The Secret to Creating Infinite Opportunities
to Grow Your Small Business**

Scott Grates

Referrals Done Right: The Secret to Creating Infinite Opportunities to Grow Your Small Business
Copyright © 2024 Scott Grates

No part of this book may be reproduced or transmitted in any form or by any means, electronic or mechanical, including photocopying and recording, or by any information storage or retrieval system, except as may be expressly permitted by the 1976 Copyright Act or in writing from the publisher. Requests for permission should be addressed to storybuilderspress@gmail.com

Published by Storybuilders Press

Hardcover: 978-1-954521-39-1
Paperback: 978-1-954521-42-1
eBook: 978-1-954521-40-7
Audio: 978-1-954521-41-4

This book is for the bold, courageous, hardworking, inspired optimist who had a 10,000 foot vision of better serving those around them with a business of their own. I am glad you took the leap, and excited to provide a parachute.

CONTENTS

Chapter 1: David and Goliath 11
Chapter 2: Don't Just Get Lucky. Get Strategic 27
Chapter 3: From One Underdog to Another 43
Chapter 4: The Heart of the Matter 57
Chapter 5: The Infinite Referral Advantage® 72
Chapter 6: The Income Advantage: Small Business Owners 85
Chapter 7: The Impact Advantage: Schools 105
Chapter 8: The Involvement Advantage: Service Organizations 122
Chapter 9: The Introduction Advantage: Star Customers 138
Chapter Ten: The Influence Advantage: Social Engagement 155
Chapter 11: Maintaining Your Infinite Referral Advantage® 172
Chapter 12: Grit and Faith 195

    Acknowledgements 208
    Endnotes 209
    About the Author 210

CHAPTER 1

DAVID AND GOLIATH

∞

One small stone. That's all it took to defeat a giant. You've heard the expression—David and Goliath, and you probably know the biblical story.

Goliath was a giant. Depending on your understanding of ancient measurements, he was huge, somewhere between seven to ten feet tall. Not only that, he was loud. He stood taunting his opponents, daring them to fight him. Decked out in heavy armor, he was the veritable "Iron Man" of the Bronze Age. He *sounded* unbeatable. He *looked* unbeatable.

So day after day, the armies lined up in battle, Goliath taunted, and his opponents withered.

Until David showed up.

David was a young shepherd, but he wasn't helpless. He'd fought his share of battles protecting his sheep. He had the scars and calluses to prove it. He also had a different perspective. Where the cowardly armies saw an unbeatable giant, David saw an opportunity.

He went to the stream and picked up five smooth stones.

He dried them off and weighed each one in his hand.

He pulled out his sling and seated one stone in the worn leather pouch.

He listened to the taunts of the giant.

He tossed out a few taunts of his own.

He looked at his objective. (I'm not sure how big the forehead of a giant was, but it probably made a nice target.)

Around and around went the sling. The tendons and muscles on his arms flexed.

The rope that held the leather pouch cut through the air with a slicing whine.

The giant rushed toward the boy. The boy rushed right back.

And then, just like he'd done many times before, he let go of one end of the rope and watched the rock launch toward Goliath. He probably was laughing at this small boy right up until the stone drilled him between the eyes.

Can you imagine the sound a ten-foot-tall giant makes when he hits the ground? I'm sure it wasn't quiet. (If you want to read the rest of the story, you'll see it's pretty crazy. You don't have to be religious to enjoy its audacity. Look up 1 Samuel 17 for what David did after Goliath fell.)

David won. Goliath lost.

Game over. Or did the game just begin?

ONE OF US IS GOING DOWN

You may be wondering why I opened with that story. The reason is simple: it's a fantastic metaphor for what you may be feeling. Here's what I assume to be true about you. You picked up this book because you own or work in a connection-based business. Like me, your business may be anchored to a geographic location. You may have relationships with other businesses in your area and have connections with industries that bump up against your own.

You may also feel a bit like David. I sure did when I got started.

I had few connections. Few tools. Only a handful of skills. But a lot of ambition and belief.

When I looked around though, I saw more than a few Goliaths. I'm in the insurance industry, so there were other agents who had been doing it longer than me. Other brands that were bigger than me. Other options that could compete with me. Goliaths loomed everywhere.

Like in the story above, they all seemed to have bigger, better resources, positions, track records, and reach.

And yet, I knew that I had what it took to make a difference.

Since you're reading this book, I'm guessing you can relate.

Like David, you feel small, perhaps underprepared, understaffed, and if you're honest, possibly a little inexperienced and underwhelming. You have a vision for what you want to accomplish in your business, and yet, if you get a moment to stop scrambling and look around, all you see are giants. These giants can outspend you, outmaneuver you, outstaff you, outmarket you, and maybe even outwait you. That's why you keep your head down and control what you can.

Every day you go into the office early, flip the lights on, roll up your sleeves, and get to work. Like David, you grab your "five smooth stones" and put them in your pouch. They don't seem like much, but they are all you've got. Then you start making calls. Looking for business. Turning over rocks. Making the asks.

One of these things has to work, right?

Here's the truth: If you are a David, you don't have to compete head-to-head against Goliath.

For your business to succeed in an industry full of Goliaths, you need to get strategic.

If you read the rest of the David and Goliath story, you know there were other forces at work, and David didn't just get lucky with a small stone and a sling.

He was being strategic, and it paid off. Big. The same is true for you. For your business to succeed in an industry full of Goliaths, you need to get strategic.

Fortunately, I can show you how.

BIG DREAMS, LITTLE TRACTION

"I will own and operate the most dominant insurance agency in my market."

I wrote these thirteen ambitious words on a card in front of me at a four-hour presentation outlining the path required to become an insurance agency owner. They felt bold. They *were* bold. I didn't know how I was going to make it happen, but in that moment, hopped-up on the entrepreneurial energy around me, I knew *I was going to make it happen.*

But let me back up a second.

I didn't set out to change relationship marketing. That day I had no plans of writing this book. I had no clue I would start Insurance Agency Optimization, a coaching and consulting business serving thousands of insurance professionals. I only knew one thing: I needed a job, and I needed it quickly.

The ball had recently dropped to begin 2009—thank goodness. If there was ever a year I was glad to leave in the rearview mirror, it was 2008. The global financial meltdown had cost me my job in the banking industry, and I hadn't exactly squirreled away a fortune to carry me and my young family through hard times.

Losing my job hit deeper than the bottom of the bank account though. It left me questioning the way forward. I was ready for a change, but a change to what? Sitting in another cubicle building someone else's dream from eight to six, hoping traffic cooperated and I'd make it home before my kids went to bed?

Visions of independence and success started to fill my head. I began envisioning a life of freedom and success—free from the golden shackles of the corporate world, controlling my time, not answering to a boss, and reveling in my financial independence.

So I began researching options, and I found insurance. That was something I could do.

Those visions brought me to a white-walled, industrial-carpeted, windowless conference room where for four hours, I met with other wide-eyed optimists, listened to success stories, and learned the path required to become an insurance agency owner.

Inspired by hope, I grabbed the paper name tent before me and scribbled these words: *I will own and operate the most dominant insurance agency in my market.*

Maybe I was a bit crazy; maybe it was the contagious energy in the room. Certainly, I was naive. Despite my accolades as a top producer in banking, selling insurance was uncharted territory. I didn't even know the first thing about insurance. Come to think of it—I was a novice at entrepreneurship too.

I hadn't owned a business, hired employees, created a marketing plan, dealt with human resource issues, or managed profit-and-loss statements. All I had was a wife, two babies at home, and no income to support them. I never really considered myself to be a salesman. Sure, it's what I always *did*, but never who I *was*. I just loved people. I also loved offering loads of personal value. Turns out, the insurance company I was there to learn about is also people-centric and provides tremendous products and services.

This had to be the way to the life I envisioned!

Rare are the moments when my wife and I sit in silence. However, for the initial twenty minutes of our car ride home after that meeting, that's what we did. Each of our minds raced a mile a minute, in different directions, but neither of us spoke.

My wife, who taught school for over twenty years, is conservative by nature. To her, *risk* is a bad four-lettered word. Finally, she broke the silence.

"You are going to do this, aren't you?"

"Hell yeah, I am!"

See, I'm a gambler, a dreamer, the type who looks risk in the eye and wonders why others are so scared.

I was already off dreaming of dominating a market that was controlled by knowledgeable, experienced, well-known, and well-funded behemoths, and I didn't even have my insurance license yet.

I told you I was naive.

While I didn't know where to start, I knew I *had* to start. The gun had been fired, and it was time to run.

Soon my days were filled with business planning—securing an office location and completing its build-out; buying furniture, signage, and phone systems; recruiting and hiring; licensing tasks and advertising. Each time I crossed three items off my to-do list, four more appeared.

Over the next six months, I sought relationships with people ten steps ahead of me on this journey. I pleaded with every insurance agency owner within a two-hour radius to help me. I begged for guidance, tips, tricks, systems, processes, and insights into anything they could offer that would help jump-start my launch.

Every day I packed peanut butter and jelly sandwiches and bottles of tap water into my two-door Honda Civic, which had no power seats, windows, cruise control, or even a CD player, and I prayed I'd have enough gas to make my visits and get back home.

Thanks to my generous colleagues in the region, my marketing plan was ready by the time my opening day arrived—or so I thought.

I heard two consistent messages in all my meetings: "Know your marketing numbers" and "Don't reinvent the wheel" (the "wheel" being the traditional marketing methods). The part about knowing the numbers was crucial and still is today. However, as an out-of-the-box thinker trying to follow along with those messages, it didn't take me long to learn that the "wheel" desperately needed some realignment.

Taking on a contrarian view is better than just getting an answer and running with it. *Question everything. Don't ask questions looking for an answer, but ask questions to obtain new wisdom.* When you are willing to look for different answers, it can feel risky, but the rewards can be much greater and more fulfilling.

You know it too. It's probably why you bought this book. These traditional marketing methods and strategies are not only draining your bank account but draining your energy, enthusiasm, and dreams too.

Soon after I launched my business, clients didn't start streaming in my doors like I'd imagined they would. I immediately saw and felt the big, painful gap between what I knew about marketing and what I clearly *needed* to know.

Each week, when the weekly rankings were posted, I wanted to see my name at the top. And to be honest, if I'm not first, I might as well be last. I wanted and, honestly, expected that I'd be ranked first, then there'd be everyone else. But what I didn't know was at what cost and lengths I'd go to try to get there.

At the time I had no customers, lacked a personal brand, and had zero referral partners. (I told you, I was naive.) I could have taken a tortoise-like approach to slowly and steadily win this race I thought I was in, but I didn't have time for that.

I had something to prove.

So like the impulsive rabbit, over the course of the year, I slowly emptied my checking account, exhausted our savings, and leveraged credit from every institution that deemed me worthy to flood the market with ads, direct mail, and all the traditional marketing tools I could get my hands on.

By nearly the end of my first year in business, my wife and I were sitting in the basement of our home, facing foreclosure. After another long, stressful day, we had finally gotten our baby boys to sleep and could focus on the giant in front of us.

A year of constantly juggling paying certain bills one month and others the following month—mostly from lines of credit—had nearly shattered us. Visions of a potential financial breakthrough kept me going, but the reality of being broke was suffocating us, our marriage, and our family. The more debt I juggled, the more a potential financial breakthrough seemed like a mirage in the desert.

I asked my wife to sit with me for a serious talk. She knew I'd been spending and borrowing, but I wasn't sure she knew the full extent of our current reality. To say my pride was bruised is an understatement. I was also afraid.

As we settled into our chairs at the kitchen table, my mind flashed back to eighteen months prior. To that silent twenty minutes in the car on the way home from the informative seminar. I knew in those moments she had been envisioning this exact situation as she worried about where this journey might take us. Now I had to tell her it had come.

I was certain the first words out of her mouth would be, "I told you so." But fortunately, my wife is much, much better than that.

She knew I was trying my best. She saw me putting in the hours, logging the miles, and shaking all the hands of everyone in our town. She also understood the task of building something from nothing is enormous—but she was still willing to bet on me while I figured it out.

"So what now? How do you plan to get us out of this?" she nervously inquired.

"I'm not sure, but there has to be a better way. I'll figure it out. I promise," I honestly answered.

So I got to work by going back to the basics of what I knew, and here's what I came up with: I started my business to make meaningful connections, to offer abundant value to my community. I didn't want to be Goliath. I wanted to be me.

I love working with people one-on-one, understanding them at a deeper level, discovering their problems, and offering real, workable solutions. My desire to grow my business as big as possible, as fast as possible, forced me to work contrary to my core beliefs. Trying to copy the giants was inauthentic. It only ended up making life uncomfortable and success improbable.

The day you open your small business, an invisible two-ton boulder gets placed at your front door. It represents everything you want your business to be: an incredible team working with you whose strengths represent your weaknesses and vice versa, lifelong clients, an unshakeable revenue stream for you and your team, and so many referrals that you'll never have to go looking for business again.

In order to achieve all you envision, you have to move the boulder. So what's the best way to get it moving from where you are to where you want to be?

You can do two things. Option A is to pump yourself with steroids to give you instant, unnatural strength to shove that boulder enough for customers to squeeze in the door. This could be things like purchasing leads from internet vendors; hiring telemarketers for cold calls; flooding the market with direct mail, billboards, and TV and radio advertisements; and creating high-priced SEO plans.

Or you can focus on diet, exercise, and daily strength training to slowly push that boulder away until it's gone for good. This is what you'll learn to do in this book.

One option creates a long-term dependency on an unhealthy solution that will destroy you eventually. The other will set you up for sustainable success. Concerning physical activity, we all know that good nutrition and fitness beat steroid injections. So why don't we follow the same principle in business?

Many entrepreneurs will spend themselves right into insolvency through quick-fix marketing schemes and fail to build the muscle required of a strong organization that can survive in any conditions.

How do I know? Because before I figured out the tools that this book holds, I did it too.

Very early in my career, a well-trained television sales representative named Amanda visited my office to offer me an "exclusive opportunity" to run two fifteen-second spots during the upcoming Super Bowl. These were regional spots, not the $114 million national ads everyone sees. Each local network receives a handful of these spots that lead up to the game and air in between quarters, not during the game itself. Regardless, a chunk of my potential customers should be tuning in.

This type of marketing went against my slow, steady, consistent approach and was well outside my budget. However, in my mind, and with Amanda's encouragement, I thought these ads could be the colossal breakthrough I was looking for. I spent over half of my annual budget on two fifteen-second advertisements.

The result? A bunch of texts from friends and family saying how cool it was that they saw me on TV.

That was it.

The ads had zero impact on my customer acquisition.

I had jumped into a crowded space where the Goliaths reigned thinking I'd come out the champion. As a result, I negatively impacted my expenses and limited my ability to operate as I should have for the remainder of the year.

While I do regret the decision, I don't blame myself for making it. I was desperate to succeed and grasping for anything and everything that seemed like it might be the thing to lever that boulder from my door faster.

Marketing is your business's lifeline, the difference between thriving and barely surviving. There's so much angst around it because so much rides on it. Marketing's aim is to create awareness, build interest, and ultimately, drive people to choose a particular product, service, or brand. It's the art of making a lasting impression and helping people realize that your service or product is exactly what they need. The ultimate goal is to create top-of-mind awareness so that when somebody does need the products or services you offer, they instantly think of you as an option.

It takes a lot of resources to create that awareness. It can take five, seven, ten, or more times for a customer to see your ad before making contact with you. The number of times varies, but the most important fact to grasp is that whatever that magic number is, it's higher than one.

So you must repeat your message until your prospective customer acts.

We turn to direct mail, internet leads, referrals, and telemarketing to help us be seen. But the key to this model is volume. For it to work well, it requires an almost constant outflow of money and energy to create, produce, and launch marketing materials each year.

Many marketing strategies might promise swift and stellar results, but the bills they rack up can be unhealthy for your bottom line.

This model works great if you are the CEO of a large corporation sitting on a mountain of cash for your advertising budget. Just spend millions of dollars every month to do it all! And they do.

The problem is, you are not that CEO. You are a small business owner with a minuscule budget compared to the big players you're competing against. You're a David in a sea of Goliaths. Attempting to win their game by outspending them dollar for dollar is impossible. You'll lose that battle every time.

I know what you're thinking: *Of course I can't do that, Scott. That's why I just do a scaled-back version of that.*

That won't work either. And if you're reading this book, you've probably realized that referrals are important, and there has to be a better way to get them.

You can't win when you fight by Goliath's rules. David won because he fought by his own rules. He leaned into his expertise, relied on his weapon of choice, and worked the situation to his advantage.

He didn't just try to get lucky; he got strategic.

THE POWER OF THE PEOPLE AROUND YOU

A major psychological shift occurs when you stop signing the backs of paychecks and start signing the front of them. You transition from getting excited about payday to stressing out about making payroll.

You're in a game where the difficulty level just skyrocketed, and if you don't level up your skills, you'll never navigate your way forward successfully or sustainably. The constant pressure acts as a catalyst, pushing you to embrace the challenges you might have avoided in more comfortable circumstances. Moments like these will break you or reveal your hidden superpowers. The reality of starting and running a business is much harder than the plug-and-play approach I was taught in any training I received after I signed my contract to become an insurance agent.

After that talk with my wife, I realized that my superpower was being brilliant at the basics. It was time to go back to move forward. I had to rely on what had helped me to win in the past.

Connecting with people individually and providing value was my long-term strength and conditioning program that would help me move the rock between my clients and myself. Humans desire meaningful relationships, and consumers are on the hunt for genuine value. While big corporations seek to do more with less and automate as many aspects of the business as possible, today, more than ever, we operate in a *connection economy*. Those who are respected and remain relevant are more referable than ever.

Building and reinforcing meaningful relationships isn't a quick fix for a marketing misstep. It's not a quick-and-easy solution for your marketing problems either. But the payoffs? A sustainable business that adds value to your life, and the lives of others, and an ever-expanding bottom line.

The old ROI (return on investment) is just a soulless math equation that doesn't always work out. It's an uninspiring approach to business.

It's your relationships that will give you the greatest return on your investment.

I saw your eyes roll after reading that. You're thinking, *I already know that meaningful relationships are a good thing.* I know that you know that too, but what are you doing to cultivate *new* relationships and *strengthen* existing ones each day? Maybe you know it, but you have some hesitancy around referrals because getting them has felt awkward for you, your customers, or worse, both.

Relationships are what will allow you to dominate in Goliath's market for the following reasons:

→ **Relationships Optimize Influence.** Creating win-win relationships impacts the next generation, enhances personal branding, develops leadership skills, and creates valuable networking connections.

→ **Relationships Optimize Involvement.** Adopting a heart of service fosters community improvement and heightens relevance, respect, and referability.

- **Relationships Optimize Introductions.** Leveraging your biggest fans creates enthusiastic advocates eager to share your business within their personal networks.
- **Relationships Optimize Income.** Relationships eliminate the need for costly mass marketing and attract ideal potential customers who are ready to buy.

What lies ahead of you in this book will teach you how to get a better kind of ROI than what traditional marketing can offer.

With consistency, this approach will allow you to build the life you want, the business you dream of, and a community of rich relationships with a reach far beyond your office walls.

To do this, you don't have to go meet every person in your city or town and give them a pen with your name on it. You don't have to shake everyone's hand like a politician or stick business cards under the windshield wipers of every car in the parking lot. By strategically investing in relationships with just a few people, organizations, and institutions, you will create a self-perpetuating cycle of involvement and introductions that has customers walking through your doors, ready to buy.

WELCOME, UNDERDOGS!

Let the big businesses with deep pockets lean on the old ROI formulas. The new ROI is for the underdog. It's only available to the purpose-driven small business owner who lives, works, plays, and cares about the community they serve.

It is for you.

This book is the exact framework that has helped me scale my small local insurance agency in a town of 7,500 people to seven-figure revenue. It's also the framework that I've taught to thousands of small business owners and that has created a multitude of community leaders and mentors making a positive impact on thousands around them.

In *The Slight Edge*, Jeff Olson writes, "Small, seemingly inconsequential actions done consistently over time will create massive results."[1] I know this is true because I've done it and I've seen it. You don't have to be a type A extrovert (and if you are, that's okay too). You don't have to have tons of cash to spend on marketing. You don't have to be educated in the Ivy League. You can just be a normal person, like David, who did something comparatively small and won the fight. Doing small actions consistently will enable you too to win each battle and not lose your mind, money, or soul.

Welcome to the wonderful world of the new ROI, where keeping customers in and competitors out is just another day at the office!

CHAPTER 2

DON'T JUST GET LUCKY. GET STRATEGIC.

∞

Like many clients I help in my consulting business, Gina was full of ambition and ready to do whatever it took to get her dream of owning a small business off the ground. After investing the time and training required to become an insurance agent, she rented a storefront and turned on the "Open" sign.

Gina was determined to ensure the growth of her business was not only profitable but also sustainable. She believed in and invested in traditional marketing. After only a few years as a business owner, Gina was feeling the full effects of burnout. She felt like she didn't have a second to spare, and the money she was putting into marketing wasn't creating the profits she had hoped for.

In fact, after another excruciating day filled with meeting prospects, interviewing customer service reps after receiving her administrator's letter of resignation, navigating the phone lines herself as calls came in, coordinating a time when the heating and cooling guy could come check the furnace, and waiting on hold for the IT person to come check on her laptop, she sat down to do the bills.

Her gross revenue was looking good, as usual. But if the same volume of marketing leads were purchased, in a few short months, she'd be paying out more money than she'd make. She needed to increase profits—fast. But how could she reach more people if she couldn't spend more money? And how in the world could she hire more help if she couldn't pay them? How could she hustle more when she was already short on time?

Realizing that she'd missed dinner with her family hours ago, she gathered her things to go home. With slumped shoulders, she reached over and clicked the "Open" sign off.

THE WEARING OF THE HATS

Let's take a quick roll call. Name the person managing each of the following departments for your business. Jot down their names in the margin as you read.

1. **Human Resources (HR)**—manages recruitment, employee relations, benefits, initial training, paid time off, and terminations.
2. **Finance**—handles financial planning, budgeting, accounting, payroll, bookkeeping, paying bills, and financial reporting.

3. **Marketing**—focuses on promoting the company's products or services, developing marketing strategies, and planning and participating in networking and community events.

4. **Sales**—responsible for consistently selling the company's products or services to customers.

5. **Information Technology (IT)**—takes care of the company's technology infrastructure, including hardware, software, and network systems.

6. **Customer service/support**—handles customer inquiries, complaints, and support for products or services.

7. **Legal**—handles legal matters, contracts, and corporate compliance and stays up to date with laws and regulations.

8. **Public Relations (PR)**—manages the company's public image, handles media relations, and promotes and protects the brand.

9. **Administration**—takes care of administrative tasks such as office management, facilities, and support services.

10. **Training and development**—focuses on long-term planning, business strategy, and development to ensure future growth through employee training.

I'm willing to bet that as you review your list of managers running each of those ten departments for your business, you see your own name listed at least seven times. (And if you aren't listed as the direct manager for a department, it's likely you have oversight or specific tasks within it.) The bottom line is, you wear many hats. Like Gina. Like I used to.

Large competitors have multiple people within each of those departments. The VP of marketing doesn't get interrupted by a service representative needing help with a customer's billing issue or then have to interview a job candidate before personally making sales calls.

The VP of marketing should have a laser-like focus on marketing all day, every day. They will *collaborate* with leadership within the sales, finance, strategy, and development departments, but they never have to do those jobs.

I'm going to take a wild guess that you do not share the same luxury.

Without the ability to lean on multiple department heads, or even other employees in some cases, the small business owner like you is forced to work more like a firefighter does than an executive.

Each day your attention gets diverted to the things that are most urgent or pose the biggest threat to your business. Exactly what that fire is will vary from day to day, and then there are always your own job responsibilities to fulfill.

Did all that hit a little too close to home? Good. Then you're in the right place.

Most small business owners enjoy taking the lead and being in control. We are a driven bunch, we love our people and our community, and we are a fairly competitive bunch too. So it's simply not in our nature to step back to allow another person to take the lead.

One of the many problems this creates is that it dilutes our focus, and diluted focus always yields diluted results.

By wearing so many hats and simply putting out fires, your focus always stays on the present. There is no time for future planning or preparation.

All the hats can cause other problems when it comes to marketing, such as the following:

1. **Limited expertise.** When you are stretched too thin, you don't have the time or energy to fully understand the nuances in the digital marketing space, nor do you have the time to gain the skills and knowledge necessary to create and execute an effective local campaign. This can lead to missed opportunities to reach the audience you so desperately want to connect with.
2. **Burnout and stress.** The more stressed you are, the less creativity you have. There's no way you'll have the brain power necessary to come up with your next great promotional idea when you're running on empty.
3. **Inadequate planning.** When you don't have enough time to create an in-depth marketing strategy, it's easy to do what the Goliaths do and put everything you can into the traditional marketing model.

THE TRADITIONAL MARKETING MODEL

When you're already overwhelmed by everything you're doing on a daily basis, you don't have the time to learn or plan a new strategy to get the results you want. It becomes easy to fall into the trap of continuing to default to the "tried and true" method of marketing. But when you rely too heavily on the traditional marketing model, you've unwittingly sentenced yourself to a life on the hamster wheel. Let me explain.

Traditional marketing ROI says that if I spend $5,000 on marketing, and my message reaches 3,000 people, then 150 will give me an opportunity to sell to them. Of those 150, 30 of those will convert into sales. So when you do the math, it costs $167 in marketing to close *one* sale. Now what if revenue goals required to cover monthly expenses require you to make 100 sales? You'd have to simply spend . . . $16,700. That's triple your monthly marketing budget! (Assuming you can afford to do that.)

In simple terms, marketing ROI performance is based on the number of leads (or opportunities to sell your product or service) generated by the number of dollars spent to get those leads.

In the traditional marketing model, the two primary metrics a small business owner (SBO) will look at are sales volume (how many units sold) and gross revenue (how much money those sales generated for the operating account). Then they look at team performance (how many units each person sold and how much they got paid to do so). This allows the business owner to determine each employee's return on investment. Then they look at marketing (how many leads or sales opportunities are generated by a specific marketing approach).

Gross revenue doesn't always lead to profitability.

Gross revenue doesn't always lead to profitability. If you've been around a while, you know that. The number of sales an employee makes isn't always determined by the number of leads they have. While the number of leads created by a marketing approach can be high, they can also cause the business owner to be dramatically over budget.

Take Alex, a new insurance agency owner who was eager to attract new interest and build a solid client base. He decided to invest $1,000 in direct mail marketing to send 2,000 postcards, each emphasizing the importance of protecting one's financial future through his offerings.

He was pretty pumped about the initial results when he received twenty inquiries from potential customers who wanted to learn more. When he did the math, his return on investment was only 2%.

Driven by the ambition to grow his client base even faster, Alex decided to aim for eighty inquiries a month. To achieve that new target, he decided to increase his monthly postcard budget to $4,000 per month. For a $60,000 annual marketing budget, $4,000 in one month for postcards is a ton of money. While this choice may seem logical under the old traditional marketing model, it marked the beginning of a cycle that would lead to diminishing returns over time.

DIMINISHING RETURNS

Brian is another insurance agent I know. He's also a great example of how the traditional approach to marketing can lead to diminishing returns and other problems.

Brian reached out to me in my coaching business a few years ago. When I saw his name in my inbox, I thought, *Why is he reaching out to me?* It wasn't his inquiry that was unusual. He asked me to help audit his business and give him suggestions on its inefficiencies and any areas of improvement. It was the person behind the inquiry that caught me by surprise.

I questioned whether I was confusing his name with someone else's. The Brian I was thinking of was one of the top-performing agency owners in the country. Why would he be reaching out to me?

Brian provided me with revenue and expense reports, profit-and-loss statements, and itemized breakdowns of each marketing spend. As I was scrolling through his annual production numbers,

I realized he was the same Brian, but by the time I reached the end of his numbers, my jaw was on the floor.

Brian's business looked wildly successful from a production standpoint, but it suffered from a common problem—*diminishing returns*.

Diminishing returns are the bane of productivity enthusiasts, economists, and small business owners alike. They're like getting an extra scoop of ice cream that is delightful and fun at first, but each subsequent bite brings less satisfaction as the long-term problems start stacking up. The law of diminishing returns is a constant reminder that too much of a good thing may not be so good after all.

Brian was blinded by high production numbers, awards, public recognition, and seeing his name at the top of the charts, but his profit-and-loss statement told the rest of the story. Yes, he was generating plenty of revenue, but he wasn't keeping much of it.

In my work as a consultant, I see many small business owners fall into the trap of having tunnel vision or looking one-dimensionally at production numbers. When this happens, equally important expense numbers can become overlooked and unchecked over time.

This is a common mistake small business owners make.

In an effort to drive more production, which creates higher gross revenue, they inflate their marketing budgets and payroll. This is what Brian was doing. He was spending over $5,000 per month to purchase online leads, and then another $5,000 per month on employees to work those leads.

From a marketing standpoint, the return was solid: his team was receiving hundreds of new leads and converting at the industry's average rate. However, the piece he wasn't focusing on was profitability, a crucial metric indicating the financial health of a business. Profitability involves generating positive net income while also managing resources efficiently, ensuring a positive return on investment, and positioning the business for long-term growth and success.

The expenses he allotted for traditional marketing and payroll to generate revenue far exceeded the revenue itself.

See the problem here?

Based on production reports, he was top of the rankings, but from a profitability standpoint, he was failing. Brian overspent on marketing because he was blindly focused on gross revenue.

Allow me to illustrate how this can happen in retail.

It's easy to buy something wholesale for $1 and then spend another $0.50 to advertise that you're selling for just above wholesale pricing $1.10. Then when you sell a thousand units, you've generated a lot of gross revenue, but each sale lost you $0.40.

> **Short-term solutions to long-term needs create an endless cycle of frustration.**

From a *marketing* standpoint, the campaign worked. It generated thousands of leads. From a production standpoint, it worked because you sold thousands of units. From a revenue standpoint, it generated plenty. But from a *profitability* standpoint, you lost.

Small business owners can find ways to feel successful by focusing on the wrong numbers. That's what Brian did.

While auditing his business, I realized his expensive, traditional marketing plan was a reactive approach designed to meet short-term goals. In an effort to increase production, he overspent on low-quality leads. Chasing these leads burned out the quality employees from the stressful task of trying to convert a high volume of bad leads into good customers.

Short-term solutions to long-term needs create an endless cycle of frustration. It truly is the hamster-on-a-wheel approach.

The business owner may see activity and sales happening. They may see their team keeping busy working leads and generating sales, but when the dust settles on the profit-and-loss report, there is barely enough remaining to keep the lights on.

The employees are doing their job well, and the customers are happy, but the business owner is working over fifty hours each week, spending time on team development, and focusing on customer service (add as many "hats" here as you'd like). They feel as if they're doing everything right, but they grow frustrated at seeing positive top-line results not translating into bottom-line profits.

SUCCESS ISN'T ALWAYS A GOOD THING

Success, too, can be a problem.

Wait. What?

Yes, some small business owners can be fooled by their own successes. I see it pretty often. It can offset our focus on the negative effects of our daily business decisions and cause us to miss or even ignore the losses and only celebrate gross revenue without any further examination.

This is especially true if success is coming into your business at the expense of another element in your operations that is crucial to long-term sustainability. Goliath-sized companies can advertise with consistency, month after month and year after year, without any impact on the CEO. They have deep pockets and a marketing department and sales force, so it can work. The focus is on high numbers.

But for many small businesses, playing this game often contributes to their own failure. Thirty-eight percent of small businesses fail due to a lack of capital, and countless more fail from burnout.[1]

Success can also bring diminishing returns on your mental and emotional state. It is one thing to write a marketing strategy in a business plan and a whole other thing to have to produce results month after month from scratch. This grind will begin to edge out the people and priorities that led you to start your own business in the first place. It's no easy feat to leave behind corporate jobs, security, and benefits to start out on your own. You undoubtedly did it with not only a great product or service in mind, but with people and your community in mind as well. You wanted to make a difference in your own life, the life of your family, and the lives of others in your area too. There is simply no time for impact like this when you're logging miles on the hamster wheel.

NO PLAN B

I was nowhere near as "successful" as Brian when I realized something needed to change in my business or I was going to fail and take my family and team down with me.

Fortunately, the scrappy, hustling, resourceful mindset I developed growing up in a low-income household gave me some valuable insights that I've used while growing my small businesses.

Because of my own experience, I was keenly aware that the livelihoods and families of others depended on the success of my business. Knowing that my team members were doing the best they could to keep things afloat at home motivated me more than anything else.

There were only four of us early on, and my three employees were willingly working for less money than they could have earned elsewhere. They bought into our value-based mission to serve our customers differently than the competition. They stayed late and took appointments in the evening hours as needed. I promised them that if they bet on me early, I'd make it up to them once we were established and profitable. I wanted to do my best to ensure the business was healthy and sustainable to provide them with opportunity and security.

Growing up poor also taught me that you don't always get the luxury of a Plan B. So being effective and resourceful in your Plan A is essential. It was resourcefulness that enabled me to work two jobs during high school, lead sports teams, and start a home-based business while I was in college. But for some reason, my resourcefulness took a back seat to the approach that everyone else was using. Instead of asking my typical questions, I grabbed onto the "tried and true" model and ran with it.

The major problem I had when I followed the traditional marketing model and what I'd learned from others was that all the initial ROI was negative.

My first year looked like this:

- Send direct mail ($.18 in return for each dollar)
- Purchase online leads ($.63 in return for each dollar)
- Hire a telemarketer (factored in with online leads)
- Run ads in newspapers and on radio ($.07 in return for each dollar)
- Rent billboard space ($.12 in return for each dollar)

→ Ask people I knew to connect me to people they knew ($26 in return for each dollar)

→ Pray that people noticed or cared (unlimited anxiety with no dollars left to spend)

My marketing plan would only be successful if I could last long enough to turn new customers into repeat customers, increase my budget, and expand my team. Eventually, the repeat business would generate enough revenue to offset the negative return on investment from advertising and marketing.

My problem? I wasn't going to last that long.

After one year in business, I'd spent over $60,000 on advertising and marketing. My wife and I were talking about foreclosure, and my whole dream was on the ropes.

When expensive, traditional marketing plans missed the mark for my business, I took it personally. Not only did it hurt the business, but it also had a negative impact on my team. The profits I'd promised them for sticking with me weren't there. I knew I needed to be creative and resourceful, which would help me keep my house, pay my team, and build my dream.

The traditional marketing method I followed was not just hurting our bottom line. Worse still, this model definitely wasn't bringing value to anyone—not me, not my team, not my community.

After digging into my marketing numbers, I could identify only one single source of positive ROI in my whole marketing strategy—referrals.

Not only were referrals the lone positive ROI in my plan, but they were thirty times more lucrative than the next best performer! I did not receive an MBA from The Wharton School, but I did learn "greater than" and "less than" in elementary school. It often cost me nothing to receive a referral, and the conversion rate (turning a prospect into a customer) on referrals was the highest of any category.

In his book, *The One Thing*, Gary Keller encourages readers to ask themselves the focusing question: "What's the ONE thing I can do such that by doing it, everything else will be easier or unnecessary?"[2]

So I began to ask myself, "What's the one thing I can personally do at such a high level that by doing so, everything else falls into place and almost nothing else matters?"

My answer was to consistently provide sufficient, sustainable sales opportunities for my team. To do that, I needed a laserlike focus on providing a consistent and potentially endless flow of opportunities, and those opportunities looked like referrals.

So I rallied the troops to further discuss the changes that were about to transpire.

I was at a financial crossroads. I told my team that we'd be "burning the boats," meaning we were going to move away from only using traditional marketing and focus all our energy on relationship optimization. We were either going to win or die trying, but retreating back to the boat (of traditional marketing) wasn't going to be an option. I simply couldn't afford it.

From that moment on, I stopped being the VP of seven different departments and locked in on just two: (1) recruitment and development of quality employees and (2) efficient relationship-based marketing to ensure those star people have endless opportunities to shine.

But, Scott . . .

Nope! Stop right there.

I know what you're thinking. You can't take off any of your hats because you don't have the right people in place and the finances available to outsource things. Are you afraid of losing revenue by ditching or scaling back on your traditional marketing? Have you "tried it all before" and didn't see the success you wanted and stopped? Or if you're honest, do you have some major hang-ups when you think about referrals, relationships, and networking?

Before you shut the book, let me tell you what I told my team all those years ago:

Keep an open mind, and stick with me.

If you're interested in creating a sustainable business and authentic, engaging relationships that increase your profitability, this is the book for you.

Once I made the decision to part ways with old-school, traditional marketing, our balance sheet became healthier than ever. Wherever you are right now, what I am going to teach you will help you make changes so yours can too.

GET OFF THE HAMSTER WHEEL

Traditional marketing will leave most small business owners either spinning their wheels or drowning in negative returns. With it, your business is not better off, and your community isn't either.

But when you amplify your relationships, you operate from a position of service, strength, and control of your future. Instead of giving your power over to the "spray and pray" approach to marketing and then waiting to see who responds, you will own your impact, your influence, and your income.

Your relationships will allow you to generate consistent referrals without even asking.

How do you know?

Because in my own business, and the businesses of those I coach, it would currently take us much more time and effort for us to *stop* getting referrals than to get more of them.

When executed with consistency, this value-driven system positions you as trustworthy, respectable, and ultimately, incredibly referable.

I'm excited to share with you my approach to establishing the kind of cringe-free relationships that help everyone involved. I won't lie to you and say you'll become an overnight success. This method takes time, but as someone who remained consistent and patient as I was building my own business this way, I can tell you, it's worth the time and effort.

And no, you don't have to be an altruist or an extrovert or give up on earning the income and having the freedom you dreamed about.

All it takes is a willingness to learn something new, a little patience, and a lot of consistency.

But first, let me tell you a little bit more about how I broke free from the hamster wheel that was dragging me down and closed the distance between my reality and my dreams.

CHAPTER 3

FROM ONE UNDERDOG TO ANOTHER

∞

On the first day of December 2009, a Tuesday, I made the 1.1-mile drive from my home to the first insurance agency I would open. Gray clouds clogged the Central New York skies. My rubber wipers squeaked as they dragged across the glass, clearing the cold drizzle from my view.

I caught a red at the only traffic light on the route, and while I waited, I switched off the music. Today I needed to be focused. I had spent the prior seven months preparing for this day, and my feelings were buzzing all over the place. It was a short, four-minute drive, but four hundred "what if" questions were bouncing in my head.

Was I excited? *Oh yeah.*

Was I scared? *You bet.*

But was I ready? *Absolutely not!*

How could I be?

Too many unknown variables were in play. What if my team couldn't handle the business? What if I couldn't help them when things went wrong? What if people didn't care about what I offered? Or what if nobody showed up or answered my calls?

The longer I *what-iffed*, the louder and more insistent the questions grew.

What if my marketing plan bombed? What if I couldn't make my first payroll? What if I couldn't pay my bills? What if my family ended up on the street, standing in front of a big, bright "Foreclosure" sign on our house?

I had to get a grip!

What were once just conference-room dream circles, big ideas from think tanks, and strategic planning on paper had all switched to real-world situations. I was no longer a planner or a dreamer. Now I was a doer. And I would either do it right or lose everything.

I turned off the car in the parking lot but stayed belted into my seat, staring at my name printed in block letters on the sign affixed to the side of the building. The letters blurred through the relentless raindrops that cascaded down my windshield. My head was spinning.

It was go time.

FIFTY-SEVEN HOURS LATER

Go time indeed. But now, fifty-seven hours later, I sat in my office in a cloudy mental haze. I hadn't slept in two nights because my stress was so high. With so much on my mind, I didn't feel up to seeing anyone—clients, prospects, or otherwise.

Unaware of my sour mood, a sharply dressed woman stepped into my office, extended her hand, and introduced herself.

FROM ONE UNDERDOG TO ANOTHER

"Hi, I'm Becky Smith."

Oh no, I thought. *Here comes a sales pitch. What will it be this time? A brand-new copier? A must-have phone system? Girl Scout cookies?*

My first two days running a small business in a small town taught me that local salespeople will sniff out burgeoning entrepreneurs like lions hunt a zebra in the savanna. After three days in business, the ratio of salespeople smelling fresh meat to potential customers interested in my services stood at about seven to one.

As the new kid on the block, a lifelong sales professional, and a fairly nice guy, I knew I couldn't reveal my feelings. So I put on my happy face, cleared off a chair for Becky to sit, and steeled myself for her pitch.

Becky did sit down, but she made no pitch. Instead, she congratulated me on having the courage to open a new business. I wasn't sure *courage* was the word I would use at this point, but I smiled my thanks at her.

With no evident agenda, Becky spent the next half hour getting to know me. She asked about my prior career, where I lived, my wife, my children, and our interests. Becky casually and naturally complimented me and occasionally offered thoughts and suggestions from personal experiences when appropriate.

Before Becky Smith walked through my door, I didn't know she existed, but we were chatting like old friends within minutes.

Soon Becky shifted the conversation to the professional relationships she had established within the area. I discovered she is intimately involved in our community and serves on several nonprofit and civic boards. As a result, Becky knows *a lot* of people, and she seemed happy to introduce them to me. Without hesitation, she offered the names of the many local leaders she was connected to and promised to keep me informed regarding future charitable events, marketing opportunities, and networking functions.

By the time Becky was done talking, my head was spinning—but in a good way this time. She had rattled off a dozen names of people and opportunities I should know about. And the craziest part was, I still had no clue what she did for a living.

When she stood to leave, Becky handed me her business card and said, "Oh, by the way, I own Accent Brokerage just down the road."

Becky was a realtor by profession, but on that particular evening, she didn't come by my office looking for referrals or help to snag new clients. That day Becky's sole agenda was to become my friend.

One month later, Becky stopped by again. This time she brought Travis, the owner of a local collegiate summer league baseball team, to introduce to me. The following month, Becky sent a handwritten card in the mail:

Dear Scott,
Thank you for meeting with me. I wish you much success in your new venture.
Your friend,
Becky

A month later, she introduced me to Grant, her biggest client, who needed someone to review his insurance. Then she connected with me on social media. Soon after she commented on our business's posts and shared my content. The very next month, Becky asked if I wanted to collaborate on a community event.

Over the next year, Becky sent invitations to civic organizations' functions, unique holiday gifts, and most welcome of all, unflagging support for any agency initiative we undertook.

During all this time, she never once asked me for referrals. Becky arrived with a servant's heart, offering to help a fellow business owner gain traction. Every interaction was about how she could help me get to the places I so desperately wanted to go. Becky's only priority was adding abundant value to my life. She never pitched her business or asked me for anything in return for all her support and guidance.

Meanwhile, I was pushing my insurance company for all I was worth. You would think that the sharp distinction between Becky's and my approach to business would have been clear. But it wasn't.

You see, you can't read the label when you're trapped inside a bottle. And I was trapped in the old ways of thinking about marketing, business development, and return on investment.

During my first year in business, I hyperfocused on generating revenue at any cost. I constantly took wads of money from my left pocket to invest in marketing schemes, only to put less money into my right pocket when I was done. Older, wiser, more seasoned insurance agents urged me not to reinvent the wheel, so I didn't. They all led modestly successful enterprises, so they couldn't be wrong . . . could they?

Throughout that year, I relentlessly focused on being successful, cranked out my marketing materials, and ran my plan, while periodically, Becky Smith would show up to talk and be helpful.

Then something magical happened. After several months of Becky consistently pouring value into my life, I happened to sit down with a customer looking to downsize her home.

Without thinking much about it, I asked her, "Do you already have a realtor in mind?"

She explained that it had been twenty-five years since her last real estate transaction, and she had no one.

Before my customer even finished speaking her thoughts, I jumped in with, "Oh my gosh, I *have* to introduce you to Becky Smith. You will love her. She's my favorite realtor in the community!"

And that's when it *finally* clicked for me.

THE LAW OF RECIPROCITY

At that moment, like Isaac Newton discovering gravity under the apple tree, another kind of law hit me on the head. It's called the *law of reciprocity*.

The law of reciprocity is a social psychology principle that states that people tend to respond to a positive action with another positive action. Put simply, when someone does something nice for us, we feel a psychological urge to return the favor. This principle is deeply ingrained in human social interactions and crucial to building and maintaining relationships.

> **Put simply, when someone does something nice for us, we feel a psychological urge to return the favor.**

Because the law of reciprocity is so fundamental to our human nature, we rarely think about it but use it all the time. Let me offer some examples:

Many businesses offer free samples or tastings of their products. Giving customers a small taste of their offer triggers the reciprocity principle, encouraging them to purchase the goodie. During holidays or special occasions, people exchange gifts. The act of giving a gift often prompts the receiver to reciprocate with a gift of their own.

Social media platforms often use features like Likes, Comments, and Shares. When someone engages positively with our posts, we feel inclined to reciprocate by engaging with their content.

The law of reciprocity is a powerful social force influencing human behavior across various contexts, from marketing strategies to everyday social interactions. Granted, I wasn't defining this as a scientific law the day I sat in my office with my client. I was simply excited to potentially help somebody who had helped me.

Remember that uncomfortable but necessary conversation my wife and I had about finances (or lack thereof) at the end of my first year in business? She had posed two questions: "So what do we do now?" and "How will you get us out of this situation?"

It turned out that the solution had been under my nose since my third day in business: take a page from Becky Smith's book. What if, like Becky, I poured into a network of key relationships within my community and asked for nothing in return? What if I didn't consider every conversation a potential business deal? What if I consistently made meaningful contacts to remain top of mind? What if I just helped and encouraged people every chance I got? Would I, like Becky, find that good things came back to me?

I would indeed.

INVISIBLE RESULTS

What I'm recommending is a long-term, human-centered approach to small business marketing. You can't check your numbers daily, or you'll go crazy. With relationship marketing, it could take a year of nurturing a single relationship before you get one referral. That's okay. Just because something may not pay off immediately doesn't mean that it never will.

What you're after here are what I call *invisible results*. You cannot see them because they are happening below the surface. The Chinese metaphor of the bamboo seed is a great illustration of this. When the seed goes in the ground, there are very few visible signs of growth for not just one or two years but for a full five years. Then its growth is tremendous, growing up to ninety feet tall in just six weeks. The plant can support its height and weight because for five years, that seed had been growing roots underground to support the growth that was to come. The unseen, invisible work is what not only sustains the plant's life but also causes it to grow and thrive.

But, Scott, I can't eat invisible results! Invisible results don't keep my house from foreclosure.

True. If you're in this situation, like I was, you still need to put some of your time and money into traditional marketing for now. But the key is that it is only *for now*. Combining that with the lessons of this book, you will begin to create an exit strategy from the hamster wheel for yourself by simultaneously laying the foundation of your new, improved, value-based future marketing plan.

When you switch to a relationship-driven perspective on marketing, you take the opposite line of attack upfront but keep the same retention-and-referral approach after the initial sale. (It's the old "I want to have my cake and eat it too" strategy). As I began building relationships and referrals, my sales volume decreased.

According to the traditional model, that's a bad thing. However, my profitability increased. So while I dropped thirty percent from producing over a thousand new policies annually to over seven hundred, my prospect-to-customer conversion rates increased from twenty percent to thirty-five percent. My customers had immediate trust from referrals and weren't shopping with other competitors.

My retention rates also increased. Typically, twenty-five percent of my customers would cancel within a year of being drawn in by traditional marketing. But customers who were referred to us? Less than ten percent of them left.

And to top it all off, referrals were compounding. If the referred person had a positive customer experience, enjoyed working with us, and found value in our products and services, they were more likely to refer others. Customers who referred their friends and colleagues to us paid it forward by referring at least one person they knew without being asked.

When all the dust settled after two years of focusing on referrals only, our lower sales volume was offset by lower marketing spend. Not only was my business more profitable, but the quality of our customers also improved, which in turn positively impacted my company's culture. Employee retention rates improved as our team members found more meaning in their work, were more respected by customers, and had more fun.

LEAVE THE GRIND (AND THE CRINGE) BEHIND

Traditional marketing and cold prospecting are a grind. Not only are they costly from an advertising standpoint, but they're costly from an employee standpoint. Burnout levels are high when the only way to acquire new business is from cold marketing month after month. Employees engaged in the sales process often feel awkward asking for customer referrals too. There's nothing worse than getting to the end of these conversations and having to ask, "If this has been helpful for you, could you give me the names of some of your friends who might be interested?"

Ugh, I hate that part.

Talk about a mood killer. It could be why you haven't even been asking for referrals at all and been missing out on this source of income entirely. At this point in the conversation, these new customers don't even know if they like your product or service. All they know is, they bought it, and now they feel uncomfortable around you.

You don't want to be that business. You don't want to have those salespeople.

You don't have to be!

Like traditional marketing, the strategy I recommend encourages market diversification—using different approaches across many different outlets. To count on one market exclusively can be deadly if there is a shift in that market.

The method I'm going to teach you, which worked for me and thousands of other small business owners around the nation, focuses on building relationships in five key areas. You don't have to shake every hand, kiss every baby, or become someone you are not to make this system work for you. This systematic approach eliminates the risk of market shifts. It also allows your business to communicate with prospects and customers on various levels, preventing you from becoming one-dimensional.

But that sounds overwhelming, Scott. Do you remember what you wrote about all those hats I'm wearing?

Don't worry. It's easier than it sounds, and this book is full of small simple steps you (or someone on your team) can take consistently to set the flywheel of referrals in motion.

FIVE SMOOTH STONES FOR YOUR MARKETING SLING

When I "burned the boats" and doubled down on relationships, as I'd seen Becky Smith doing, I first began by making a list of everyone I knew. Then I started to look for themes and trends among the names. As they surfaced, I found five distinct areas where relationships had already contributed to generating referrals without being asked.

These areas were the following:

1. Small business owners
2. Schools
3. Service organizations
4. Star customers
5. Social engagement

And just like that, the *Infinite Referral Advantage*® was born.

REFERRALS DONE RIGHT

Heart

Small Business Owners

School

Service Groups

Customers

Social

To create a never-ending supply of new referrals I never had to ask for, I would identify, develop, and strengthen these critical relationships by strategically delivering value wherever I could, whenever I could.

To create a never-ending supply of new referrals I never had to ask for, I would identify, develop, and strengthen these critical relationships by strategically delivering value wherever I could, whenever I could. This resulted in meaningful connections that created loyal customers, vocal supporters of my business, and people excited to share our value with others. I was able to be myself, play on my strengths, and genuinely help others in and around my community. I got to say yes to some incredible opportunities while getting to know people on a personal level. And I got to have a lot more fun!

These five specific individuals and institutions are essential for developing your *Infinite Referral Advantage*®.

Here's why:

SMALL BUSINESS OWNERS: These people are the lifeblood of the local connection economy, but there is a real temptation to adopt a one-dimensional, transactional "I'll scratch your back if you scratch mine" method to referrals that must be avoided. With these folks, you want to make it your goal to impact them positively in many ways and do so forever.

That doesn't exactly sound easy.

Stick with me. We will unpack this key relationship in chapter 6.

SCHOOLS: The vast majority of people in schools are probably not your ideal customer . . . yet. Schools are, however, full of your future customers and potential employees. You have a wonderful opportunity to invest in your community while cultivating and educating your future customers and employees now.

That's a long time to wait, Scott.

Yes, it can be. But good things are always worth waiting for. We will talk more about this in chapter 7.

SERVICE GROUPS: As a small business owner, you probably live, work, and play in the community you serve. Leaving it better than you found it means you need to become more involved with community service groups, helping to further the mission of a group with the intent of making a positive impact.

How do I find the time to do this, Scott?

I get it—we're all busy. But there are ways to get involved without overcommitting. There's more to this discussion, which we will cover in chapter 8.

Star customers: Focusing on providing the highest level of service to your customers and committing to putting their best interests above your own will build an unpaid marketing team of star customers eager to share their positive opinions and experiences with others in their networks.

I'm not good at asking my customers for referrals.

When you focus on adding value the way only you can, you'll see how easy it can be to get referrals with minimal effort. Chapter 9 will tell you everything you need to know about maximizing these relationships without awkward asks or cringy conversations.

Social engagement: Focusing on becoming more socially active, engaged in your community, and leveraging that activity on social media will allow you to authentically build a brand you're proud of and support the community you serve.

But, Scott, I'm a total introvert.

So am I! Chapter 10 will teach you how to mix business and pleasure to grow your brand in a way that feels more like gaining friends than followers.

With consistency and time, you will have authentic, value-driven connections with people in your community that will become the foundation of a marketing strategy that is sustainable, not soul-sucking or cringe-inducing, and generates infinite referrals without being asked.

It won't be easy at first, but what part of running your own business is? What it will be is more rewarding and profitable; and you'll probably find it a lot more natural and comfortable as well.

CHAPTER 4

THE HEART OF THE MATTER

∞

As a guy who cut his teeth in retail sales during the 1990s, I'd internalized the mantra beaten into young sales pros like me, which was to "turn and burn." We were told to pound the pavement. Drive for dollars. Dial for dimes. The number of customers we talked to outweighed the importance of getting to know much about them aside from how much money they were going to spend when we closed the deal.

Need to employ a deceptive sales tactic? No problem! Don't let ethics stand in the way of winning your daily quota. Go somewhere and "talk to the guy in charge," and come back with your best and final offer to pressure the heck out of them.

Get used to it, kid. That's just sales for ya.

I hated every minute of it!

Fortunately, I knew it didn't have to be this way. I saw the right way to be a salesman in my very first sales job working in a local furniture store. We all worked on straight commission, and if we wanted to eat, we had to make sales. While the rest of us waited to swoop in on customers and make a sale, Morrie would be dashing around the floor from personal customer to personal customer. Oftentimes these customers actually came in and either bypassed me and the other salesmen directly, or they asked one of us to find Morrie for them. I watched his interactions with genuine fascination.

One day I boldly asked Morrie how he managed to have so many personal customers. His response was priceless:

"If you're serious about this business, don't focus on the numbers, focus on the people. When you truly care about helping the people, they'll care about helping you."

This very same approach showed up many years later when Becky Smith walked into my agency.

Am I a salesman? I suppose you might say I am because people buy things from me. I've closed tens of thousands of sales throughout my career, but my approach is best described as educating, not selling. Best of all, my approach has been validated by the infinite introductions and referrals I receive from connections and customers who know I'm the guy who can solve their friends' and families' insurance needs.

You can implement the same approach to strengthen existing relationships, add an abundance of value, maintain consistency, leverage your small network to increase prominence, and ultimately, receive hundreds (if not thousands) of referrals without asking!

Oh, you may not improve on your revenue goals this quarter, or even this year, but given enough time, you'll reap tremendous returns that are both tangible and intangible.

THE HEART OF THE MATTER

When you lead with your heart, provide abundant value, and ask for nothing in return, you will receive everything you need in abundance.

MAKING THE SHIFT

When you do the right things for the right people at the right moments, you can never be wrong. I stopped asking, "What's in it for me?" And I started asking, "How can I make a difference for others?"

Today I sell nothing. That's right. I don't sell stuff. I like to say, if you are *trying* to make a sale, you are going about sales the wrong way. Instead of making sales, I have conversations with people. I ask an insane amount of questions and listen twice as much as I speak. By doing so, I learn about their hopes and ambitions.

> **When you do the right things for the right people at the right moments, you can never be wrong.**

Once I identify someone's need, I simply offer the solution that best helps them address that need. Some people will see the value and take action on what I suggest, but others won't. Either way, as a sales professional, I have done my job. The goal is not to get somebody to buy something but to allow them to make a well-informed decision. And if their decision is to wait, that's okay—you've established the relationship, and the fortunes are always found in the follow-ups.

Early in my career, I asked two questions:

1. How do I make more sales?
2. How do I increase revenue?

I don't ask those questions anymore. Today I ask two different questions:

1. What matters to you?
2. How can I add value to your life?

Once I changed my approach, I felt like a huge weight had been lifted off me. I no longer felt pressured to move quickly and inauthentically using cold strategies. Instead, I sought relevant relationships by genuinely offering to help others while expecting nothing in return. I was now operating from a position of strength.

I was David armed with a sling and my five smooth stones, not David trying to maneuver an unwieldy sword against an enemy many times his size. Now I couldn't lose.

"THE VALUE EQUATION" > TRADITIONAL MARKETING AND ROI

Back in our early twenties, my future wife, Kelly, and I received a glossy, slick marketing flier in the mail one cold, gray day. To say that the photos of deserted white sand beaches with turquoise water and clear blue sky, with cold drinks with little umbrellas, were inciting is an understatement. As we read the flier, it got even better—we could get it all for free.

This seemed like a deal we couldn't pass up! It was too cold, and we were too broke and young to resist. We booked our trip immediately.

Soon after that, we were on our first "adult vacation" together—all by ourselves in Puerto Vallarta, Mexico. We almost didn't mind staying at a cheap motel in the middle of town with no ocean view, no food or drinks included, no air-conditioning, and a pool that definitely didn't have enough chlorine.

We hadn't been conned (yet). We knew that in order for us to take the trip to Mexico for free, the resort company would pay for our flights and hotel and give us an "opportunity" to spend one of our six days at a 5-star resort getting first-class treatment in a luxurious setting like that flier showed.

What a great deal, right?

The resort we'd been permitted one-day access to was stunning. We got to experience 5-star service, gourmet food, and free drinks. We took walks on the white sand beach, and it was the first time we ever saw an infinity pool!

But (and you knew that *but* was coming) before the resort staff would give us a ride back to our stuffy room fifteen miles inland, the fine print on our deal caught up with us.

We had to sit through the time-share sales presentation.

If you've ever sat through one of those, you already knew what was coming when I said we got a deal on a free hotel and a day of pampering. If you didn't already know, you probably winced after reading that last sentence, and if you have never had the pleasure of sitting through one—*don't!* (That advice alone is worth what you paid for this book.)

Remember, Kelly and I were young, had just spent the past eight hours being treated like royalty, and we *might* have guzzled one too many free cervezas.

A sharply dressed man with a pearly white smile greeted us at the pool, and instead of driving us home, he escorted us into the hotel conference room. He was handsome, outrageously friendly, and seemingly became our new best friend after just a few minutes of conversation. We knew he was good at sales the same way he knew we were easy targets.

Even though Kelly and I solemnly pledged that we wouldn't buy anything, the salesman piqued our interest during our thirty-minute conversation. When he made the offer though, we politely explained that we were broke and ready to leave the resort.

If only it were that easy.

For the next fifteen minutes, he reviewed all the features we initially said we liked about the membership, and then he made a "special offer," making the time-share more "affordable."

"We sure do appreciate that," I told him. "But we aren't going to buy it. Can we go now?"

If only it were that easy.

The salesman excused himself. Five minutes later, he returned with his manager—another sharply dressed man with a pearly white smile and a big personality. He acted overly excited to meet us, but by this time, we weren't as enthusiastic about meeting him.

The manager spent the next twenty minutes reviewing additional benefits, including "free minitrips" we could take throughout the year. He then came at us hard with a one-time-only, decide-right-now, pressure-packed offer.

We had been trapped in the hotel conference room for an hour and a half. The cerveza had worn off, and we weren't confident the salesman (or his manager who magically showed up) would give us a ride back to our motel. Still, we refused to sign. The two men excused themselves from our table and said they had to make a phone call. We looked at each other in near despair.

Nothing about this was easy.

Ten minutes later, the salesmen returned. Both were smiling, but we weren't. They couldn't wait to share their "amazing news."

THE HEART OF THE MATTER

The manager explained that he had just called his regional VP and asked him for an enormous favor. He explained how he stuck his neck out for us because he knew how badly we wanted this time-share package. He told us he *never* asked this regional VP for a favor because this VP *never* said yes.

But the salesman had begged and pleaded for us.

"I told him if we doubled the points you receive, included the minitrips, and cut the price in half, you would sign for this today."

"If you are a hundred percent certain that they are going to make this purchase today," the regional VP had told him, "I will make a *one-time-only exception* for you. But this is the *only* time I will do this for you. Don't bother asking me for a deal like this again for a long time!"

The salesman insinuated that it could cost him his job if we didn't sign.

What could I say? We had been there for over two hours. They were our ride back to our motel fifteen miles away. The salesman had basically told us that he couldn't feed his family if we didn't buy the time-share.

"Sure," I conceded.

The time-share salesmen's sales techniques were strategically designed to tie us in emotionally and twist our kindness into a weakness. Like a chess match, the salesmen thoughtfully made each move, setting us up to step right into their trap. By the time they came back with the final "If you don't take advantage of this offer, you are crazy, and I'll lose my job" pitch, we were in checkmate.

And they knew it.

How?

Because they were professionally trained to use that same move with every single prospect, every single time. And their tactics worked.

We knew this purchase didn't make sense for us, but we got pulled into the guilt of causing a really nice guy to lose his job.

To say we felt used and manipulated is an understatement.

As much as we said we weren't interested, the two men kept telling us we were, in fact, very interested. Even though we never said we'd buy if they could get their VP to give us minitrips and cut the cost, they "stuck their necks out" to get us what we wanted. The only reason we didn't get up and leave was because they were our ride and we couldn't just call for an Uber back then.

So we signed the paperwork and finally got a ride back to our 1-star slum. We left that resort locked into an $8,000 contract plus annual maintenance fees, an absurd purchase for a couple with $93 in their checking account.

The buyer's remorse filled the stuffy vehicle as we rode along in silence, and it would eventually take countless hours of phone calls, paperwork, and money for legal counsel to break free of that deal two years later.

Kelly and I got zero value out of that deal. It was a one-sided, manipulative, exploitative transaction that left us literally holding the bill.

On that trip to Mexico, at first we felt like we were getting a lot for free, so our initial value equation of the trip was pretty high for us. Even during the time we spent hanging out at the resort for an entire day—pretty incredible for all the free fun that was had.

Making the purchase tipped our value equation in the opposite direction. The salesmen closed the deal, but none of it was worth the financial stress and the time, money, and effort we had to put into getting out of a sale we never wanted in the first place.

The easiest way to define the term value equation is to look at what someone is paying for compared to what they receive from the transaction. High value would mean that the product or service and the quality of the customer experience were all top-notch. Customers walk away feeling great about the transaction because they are happy with what they bought and were treated well by the person delivering the service or product. Consumers only focus on pricing in the absence of value.

There are two shortcuts to selling more. The first is to overspend on marketing to drive sales at the expense of profitability. The second is to drop pricing so there is no decision for the customer to make.

Imagine that you have to fly cross-country for a business meeting. Your favorite airline offers two seating options: first class for $1,200 or coach for $500. Which provides the better value?

It'd be the coach seating if we were going exclusively based on price. But remember, price only matters in the absence of value.

First-class seating comes with a wealth of benefits. You don't pay extra for checked luggage. You enjoy access to exclusive airport lounges, where you can unwind before your flight with complimentary food, drinks, and amenities. You get to board the aircraft first, and the flight attendant will hang your sports coat for you.

While everyone else has to wait an hour for a drink, you can have whatever you'd like as soon as you board at no additional cost. It'll be served in a real glass, and your dedicated flight attendant will stop others from boarding while they serve you. You get more space to stretch out and relax in larger, more comfortable seats and plenty of elbow room to work on meeting prep during the flight.

While the passengers crammed into coach decide between almonds and a granola bar, you can dive into a warm gourmet meal. You may even get fancy extras like noise-canceling headphones, luxurious amenity kits, or a hot towel. First class is all about adding that extra touch of comfort and style to your journey.

It's a 100/100 experience.

Well, there's more on that to come, but when you approach building your business less like a traditional salesman and with genuine kindness, service, and care, the value you offer becomes exponentially higher than the others, especially Goliath's. The people you interact with will not only have a great experience but they will also want others to benefit from interacting with you.

OFFERING WOW EXPERIENCES

So how do we help them have a great experience? Customer service expert Shep Hyken shared what he learned about "WOW experiences" from Paula Courtney, CEO of The Verde Group, a global market research consultancy specializing in helping businesses improve customer retention and loyalty.

He shared that WOW experiences are simply "delivering the basics consistently."[1] But I like to expand that definition a little more to "delivering value with every interaction." When you do this, you maximize the value equation.

In the value equation, the numerator is what the customer receives, and the denominator is what they pay. By packing the numerator of this equation with as many WOW experiences as possible for both acquaintances and customers alike, you will increase the value of what you offer. Ultimately, we want customers to say, "WOW, I'm so happy I do business with them!" We want those we meet to say, "WOW, I want to do business with them!" When folks are WOWed, they organically share their experience with friends and family, and unsolicited referrals start rolling into your business.

THE HEART OF THE MATTER

A person's response to each WOW experience you provide will grow exponentially. The first one gets you noticed, but anyone can do something impressive once. It's the next WOW that doubles the customer's experience. The third WOW doubles it again, and so forth. Let's take this equation and think about the experience of flying first class in terms of points.

Here is what the numerator for that experience would look like:

- → No extra charge for luggage: 1 WOW point
- → Access to airport lounge: 2 more WOW points
- → First to board: 4 more WOW points
- → Complimentary cocktail served in a real glass: 8 more WOW points
- → Bigger seats and plenty of space to relax or work: 16 more WOW points
- → A gourmet meal: 32 more WOW points
- → A hot towel to decompress during landing, and then you're first off the plane: 64 more WOW points!

Now let's add the numerator of WOW points: 127 in total. Divide it by the denominator (what you paid) of $1,200. You get 127/1,200 = 0.1058 (100) = 10.58% value. We'll round up to an 11% value.

Here is what the coach-class numerator looks like in number form:

- → Flight arrived on time: 1 WOW point
- → Cookies to choose from in addition to almonds, chips, and a granola bar: 2 more WOW points.
- → Free live TV on the flight: 4 more WOW points.

The total numerator of WOW points is 7. Divide it by the denominator (what you paid) of $500. That looks like 7/500 = 0.014 (100) = 1.4%. I'll be generous and round up here to a 2% value.

That's 11% percent vs. 2%. The more expensive option offered five times the value.

Both customers made it from point A to point B, but the first-class customer felt upbeat, positive, and energized after leaving that plane, while the coach customer was tired and frustrated, waiting for the line to move so he could get out of there.

What if that amazing day of pampering and luxury in Mexico had ended with a value-based approach? What if the salesmen acknowledged the fact that we were young and broke at that very moment but took the time to see our potential? Both Kelly and I had bright futures ahead, and we'd be making plenty of money soon.

Instead of convincing us to sign on the dotted line that day, they could have built trust and earned a promise from us—making them our first choice when we were financially prepared to make that purchase. Then, over the next year or two, the salesmen could have stayed in touch with us. Perhaps holiday or birthday cards, a personal email once in a while, updates on new opportunities, or legitimate deals. Maybe they could have sent some pictures from the resort to remind us of how amazing that day was.

Is it possible that Kelly and I would have returned to purchase from them? Would we have potentially brought family or friends with us on the next trip? Would we have been willing, perhaps even excited, to meet with the salesmen again who had stayed in touch with us? There is no way of knowing for sure. However, what I can tell you is that the "turn and burn" approach they chose, in lieu of the value-based relationship and follow-ups, guaranteed we'd never find out.

TODAY'S HOMEWORK

It is time to begin building your Infinite Referral Advantage® for yourself. The "Today's Homework" section of the remaining chapters of this book will help you do just that. After you read the chapter, I will have some simple steps for you to take to begin maximizing your advantage.

A sign in my office reads, "If you are not unique, you are weak." In our overstimulated, digitally distracted world, attention is the greatest gift someone can offer us.

What will we do with it when we finally earn a few minutes of someone's time and attention? How will we immediately prove that we provide something better than the average experience they've grown accustomed to?

It's crucial to offer a unique and memorable customer experience, one that's loaded with value and immediately positions the customers as the stars they are. Such an experience begins with knowing and being clear about your value statement. You may have heard this called a unique value proposition, or even an elevator pitch. You may have one already or may have thought about working on it but never did.

Now is the time. A value statement (or whatever name you want to call this) is an essential tool in every small business owner's toolbox. Nailing yours down, and practicing it, allows you to communicate your value, demonstrate your expertise, educate the listener, and have confidence in yourself and your business all at the same time. Not a bad result from a few minutes of their time and a couple of sentences.

So how do you create a value statement?

REFERRALS DONE RIGHT

I want you to shift your perspective for a moment. No longer are you the small business owner. You are now Goliath. Working with a $7 million budget, you are charged with creating one thirty-second advertisement that will air during this year's Super Bowl. One hundred fifteen million people will be watching. What are you going to say about your business?

Seriously, jot down your ideas for an ad. Got it?

Your Super Bowl ad will become the extended version of your value statement. You'll have shorter forms of this for specific situations and conversations of course. But for now, I want you to put serious thought into the following questions:

- What are your customers' pain points?
- What problems or obstacles do your customers face specific to your industry?

Now *amplify* those problems:

- What will happen if your customer doesn't figure out a solution to their problems?
- How much more painful will things become?

Offer a solution:

- How is your business uniquely qualified to help them?
- What can you offer that other service providers in your industry don't?

Finally, provide a call to action:

THE HEART OF THE MATTER

→ In any process, the first step is the most important. What is the very next step that your customers need to take?

Be sure to spell out each step clearly and make it easy for people to do. This piece will change the most as you work with prospects and customers during different stages of their journey.

Now bring it all together. It's okay if your first draft is ugly. Once you have a rough sketch, you can keep refining it.

CHAPTER 5

THE INFINITE REFERRAL ADVANTAGE®

∞

As small business leaders, we don't want global domination. Instead, we seek relevance within the communities we serve. So it's there that we can go to win. Our communities are our hidden advantage. Personal relationships make up the only arena where local small business owners hold the upper hand.

> **Our communities are our hidden advantage.**

I am not saying you should forgo traditional marketing completely and just start making friends to grow your business. But if you focus too heavily on traditional marketing exclusively while ignoring relationship marketing, you'll fail altogether. Let me say this loud and clear: **do not stop marketing!**

You don't have to fire your SEO agency, content writer, or graphic designer. You don't have to quit mailing flyers, buying airtime, or whatever else you're doing. You just need to create a climate where each marketing channel can flourish using the same core principles.

When you steer your marketing away from traditional marketing, you will not only eliminate the upfront costs, you will also avoid the ongoing expenditures. The ad budgets, the consultants, and the analytics subscriptions all add up, and there's no end in sight.

Establishing relevant relationships and becoming referrable trends to $0 after initial setup.

Zero dollars.

To truly connect with your audience and drive growth, you need to focus on building real, value-based relationships—not buy more ads, leverage keywords, or fill up mailboxes with marketing postcards. Relationships are what allow you to create meaningful bonds that will convert at exponentially higher rates than any impersonal marketing campaign ever could.

But relationships are hard.

When it comes to forced networking situations, I am a complete introvert. Just the thought of being in a room with thirty other people, all making small talk and smiling, makes me want to stand in the corner by myself and pound drinks to ease the pain.

So I completely understand what you may be thinking when you read the words *relationship marketing* or *connection economy*. You also may believe you don't know enough people to make this approach work. I thought the same as well. And the reality may be that you're right: you don't know enough people to make this work.

Not yet.

While everyone I work with understands the importance of relationships and sees value in this approach, not everyone is comfortable with the process, and that's okay.

THE BEAUTY OF PERSONALIZATION

The model I am going to show you is more than just good optics; it's about genuine human involvement and authentic engagement. It's more than business development; it's community development as well. The social capital you gain through relationship marketing isn't just a feather in your cap. It's an asset that can lead to tangible benefits like increased profitability and public recognition—not to discount the connections you make and the lives you positively impact—which further translate into business growth.

Beginning with today's homework, I'll guide you through the process of creating your initial list of key relationships. We'll continue to go in-depth on each component of the Infinite Referral Advantage®: small business owners, schools, service organizations, star customers, and social engagement. Then you'll learn how to optimize and manage your list to consistently show up for your key relationships, gaining momentum on infinite referrals over time.

My favorite part of the Infinite Referral Advantage® is that you can make it your own. If you're a contrarian like me, your first question would be, "Why do I have to do it this way?" But taking this information and making it your own is what makes it exponentially more powerful than any traditional marketing strategies that the Goliaths can come up with! Let's take a look at two different approaches from people I've worked with.

MIKE'S INFINITE REFERRAL ADVANTAGE®

An agent named Mike followed the three-step process to identify key relationships. He listed everyone he already had strong relationships with, started saluting and supporting the people on his list daily, and worked in four-week cycles.

Four months into the process, he was visiting one of the people on his list, a friend who worked at the local car dealership, when Greg, the general manager, walked by. Mike's buddy flagged him.

"Hey, Greg, I want to introduce you to my friend Mike. He's a local insurance agent."

On the surface, this was no big deal, but because Mike had committed to the Infinite Referral Advantage® when he returned to his agency, he did two things. First, he added Greg to his list of key relationships. Next, he took a few minutes to handwrite a card for Greg, expressing how grateful he was to meet him. Over the next few months, Mike strategically followed up with Greg to get to know him better.

One day Mike received a call from Greg asking if he sold life insurance; he did.

Greg said, "I'm working with an estate planner named Kim who said I need a specific life insurance policy. Could you help?"

Mike provided Greg with the policy he needed, then immediately added Kim—whom he had yet to meet in person—to his key relationship list. His first step to begin building that relationship? He wrote a note to Kim, thanking her for sharing the importance of life insurance with Greg.

After months of consistent follow-ups, Kim asked Mike if they could schedule a lunch. Kim's policy had always allowed her customers to choose whichever life insurance agent they wanted as part of the estate planning process. Lately, she found that many people didn't know a life insurance agent or felt that their life insurance agent was subpar.

Could Mike help? Of course he could!

Today Kim refers all her customers who need life insurance to Mike. The best part is that he's never asked for any introductions. That's the Infinite Referral Advantage® at its finest.

You probably cannot meet or know every small business owner in your community, and you definitely don't have time to invest in every service organization, so you do need to prioritize who you will initiate investing in. But that doesn't mean you have to only invest in these relationships. I want you to use the principles of this book to streamline your outreach but deepen your reach with everyone you encounter. You will be happier for it, your relationships will be stronger, and your business will flourish as well.

JIM'S INFINITE REFERRAL ADVANTAGE®

Jim made all the same mistakes I did when it came to exclusively focusing on traditional marketing during his first two years in business. I shared the Infinite Referral Advantage® with him, and he loved it! But there was one problem: Jim was uncomfortable in any social situation—forced or natural.

He had a clear vision for his business, was a masterful trainer of employees, and took great pride in implementing systems and processes—so long as he wasn't the face of it. So we asked Victoria, one of his employees, to lead the relationship marketing charge for Jim.

Victoria built a relationship-optimization process around the business using all the strategies you are about to learn. The result? Top-of-mind awareness without breaking the bank. Jim's business became well known by multiple key people in the community. He received more opportunities than ever via referrals without asking for them, and he wasn't even the person directly working the system.

This is how real relationships optimize income.

TODAY'S HOMEWORK

To begin developing your own Infinite Referral Advantage®, you need to be clear on your value statement. Go back to chapter 4 and complete that exercise now if you haven't already. Having clarity on who you are and what you offer enhances your brand's identity. It also removes the potential disruptive appearance of imposter syndrome as you pursue your referring relationships.

Next, you need to begin to identify the key relationships with individuals and institutions that you believe are a potential good source of referrals for your business. It does not mean you are *only* looking for referrals from them; that sort of relationship is not what this book is about.

Start by doing a brain dump by listing the names of individuals or organizations in your community that you know or would like to get to know. Don't worry, I'm giving you some guidance on how to do this below.

You know more people than you may think. And you're going to prove it right now. Use the following prompts to generate your list, beginning with potential key relationships you have that may not be top of mind when you consider your business, as follows:

REFERRALS DONE RIGHT

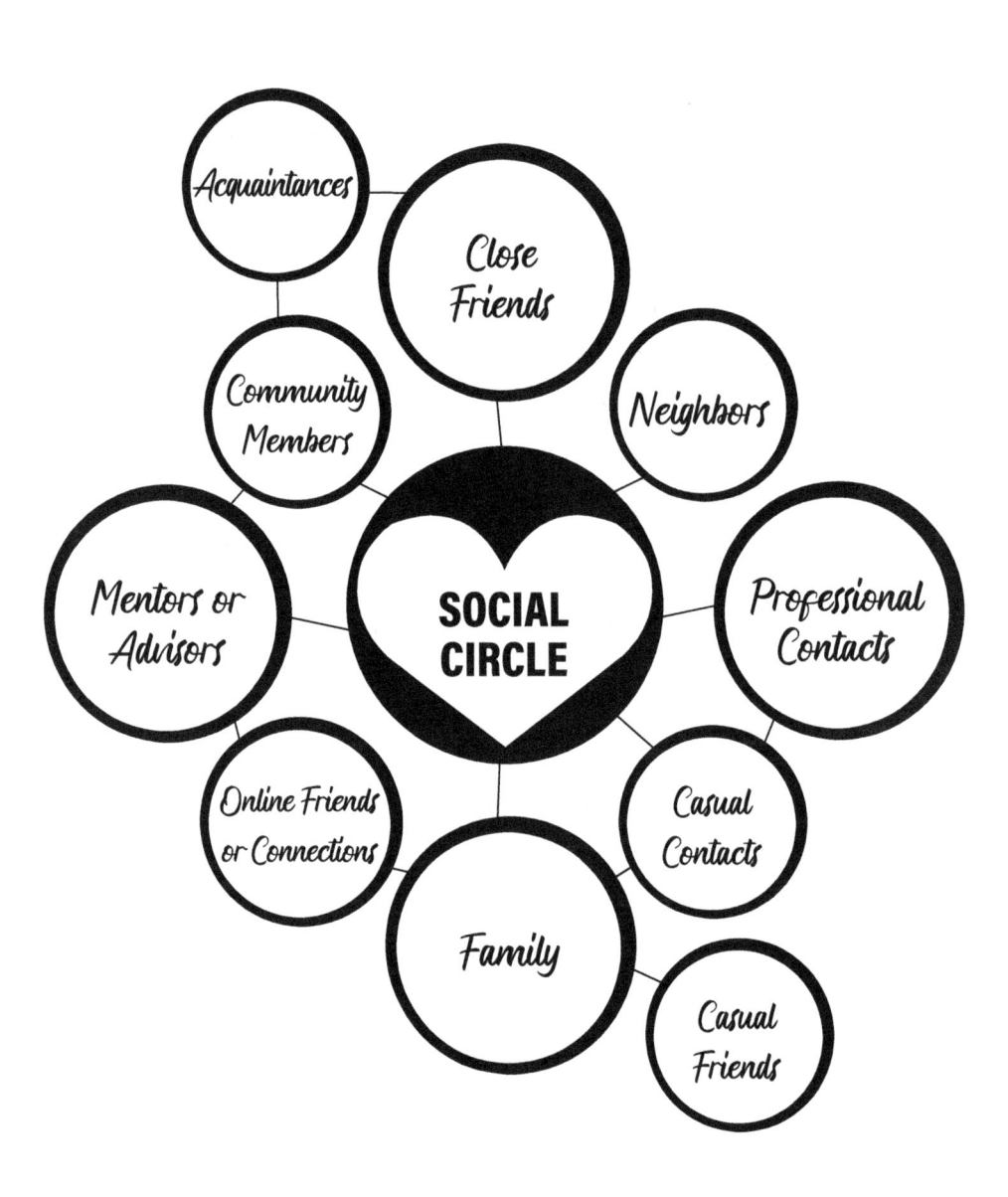

SOCIAL CIRCLE

- Acquaintances
- Close Friends
- Neighbors
- Community Members
- Professional Contacts
- Mentors or Advisors
- Casual Contacts
- Online Friends or Connections
- Family
- Casual Friends

1. **ACQUAINTANCES**

   People with whom you are familiar but may not know well. You may recognize them and have casual conversations with them, but the relationship is not deeply personal.

2. **MENTORS OR ADVISORS**

   People who provide guidance, support, and advice based on their expertise or experience. These relationships are often more formalized and focused on professional or personal development.

3. **CASUAL FRIENDS**

   Individuals with whom you have a friendly relationship but may not interact with on a regular basis. These friendships are more social and may involve shared interests or activities.

4. **CLOSE FRIENDS**

   Individuals with whom you have deeper, more meaningful connections. You share personal details and confide in each other, and the relationship goes beyond surface-level interactions.

5. **FAMILY**

   Relatives with whom you share familial bonds. This category includes immediate family members, extended family, and in-laws.

6. **NEIGHBORS**

   People who live close to you. The relationship may involve occasional interactions, borrowing items, or participating in neighborhood activities.

7. **ONLINE FRIENDS OR CONNECTIONS**

    Individuals you have connected with through social media or online platforms. The relationship may be primarily digital, and you may not have met in person.

8. **CASUAL CONTACTS**

    People you come across in day-to-day activities, such as your local barista, grocery store clerk, or gym staff. The interactions are brief and focused on the immediate context.

9. **PROFESSIONAL CONTACTS**

    Individuals with whom you maintain a professional relationship, such as clients, business partners, or industry peers. The interactions are centered around work-related matters.

10. **COMMUNITY MEMBERS**

    Individuals who are part of the same community or group, such as members of a club, church, or volunteer organization.

That wasn't too difficult. Now you have the beginning of a list. Let's go a step further. This time, consider different industries. Use the following prompts to add the people who are most likely to offer business referrals and connections:

THE INFINITE REFERRAL ADVANTAGE®

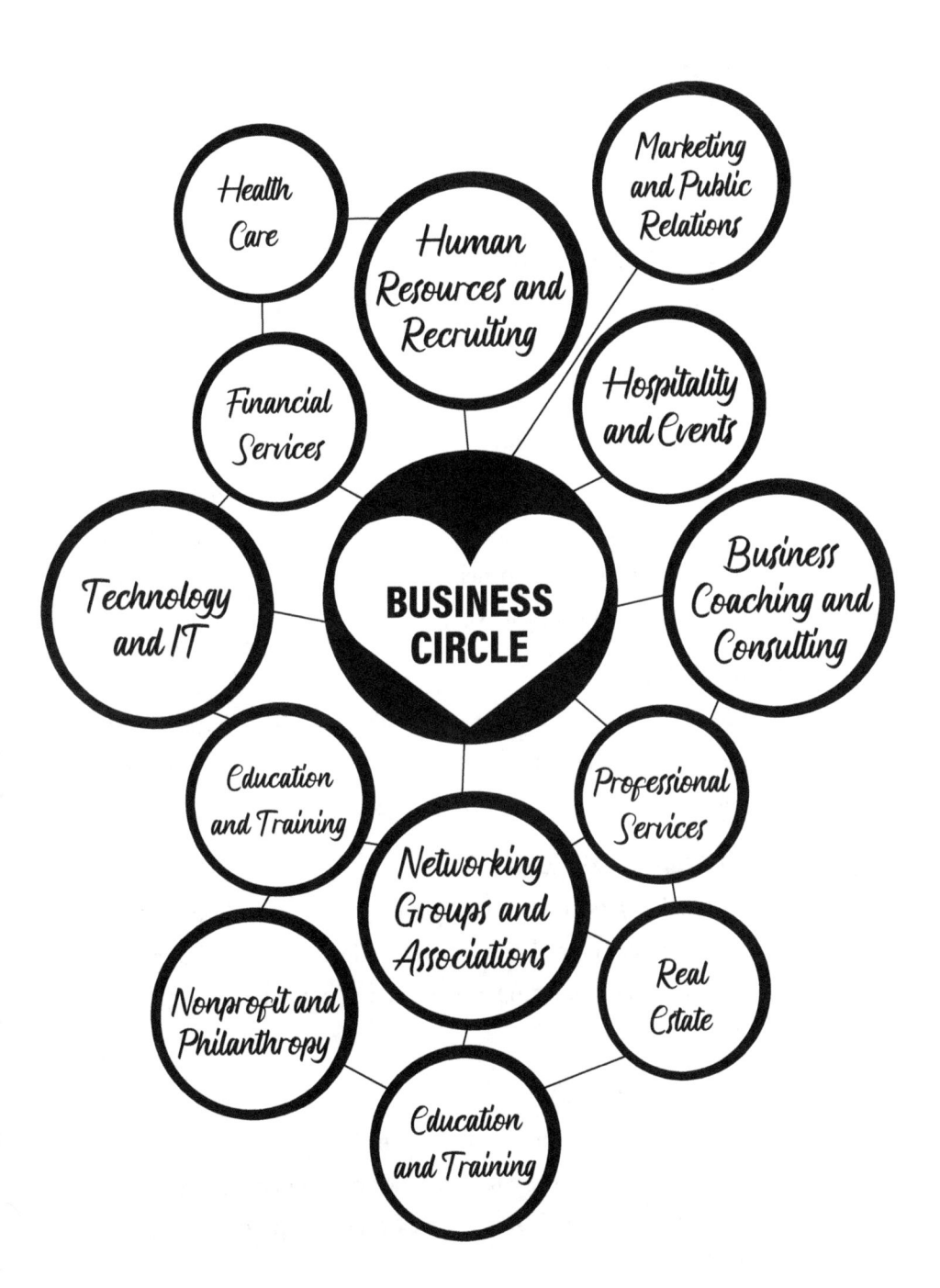

BUSINESS CIRCLE

- Health Care
- Human Resources and Recruiting
- Marketing and Public Relations
- Financial Services
- Hospitality and Events
- Technology and IT
- Business Coaching and Consulting
- Education and Training
- Networking Groups and Associations
- Professional Services
- Nonprofit and Philanthropy
- Real Estate
- Education and Training

81

1. COLLEAGUES OR COWORKERS

Individuals you work with in a professional setting. The relationship may be based on shared work responsibilities, projects, or a common workplace.

2. PROFESSIONAL SERVICES

Industries such as legal services, accounting, consulting, and marketing often involve professionals who regularly refer clients to others within their network.

3. REAL ESTATE

Real estate agents, brokers, and property managers frequently make referrals to mortgage brokers, home inspectors, contractors, and other professionals involved in the real estate transaction process.

4. HEALTH CARE

Healthcare professionals (including doctors, dentists, and specialists) often refer patients to other healthcare providers for specialized services or consultations.

5. FINANCIAL SERVICES

Financial advisors, investment bankers, and insurance agents may refer clients to professionals in related fields, such as estate planning attorneys, tax consultants, or insurance specialists.

6. TECHNOLOGY AND IT

Professionals in the technology industry often collaborate on projects and may refer clients or business contacts to specialists in areas such as software development, cybersecurity, or IT consulting.

7. HOSPITALITY AND EVENTS

Wedding planners, event coordinators, and professionals in the hospitality industry often refer clients to photographers, caterers, florists, and other event-related services.

8. BUSINESS COACHING AND CONSULTING

Coaches, mentors, and business consultants frequently refer clients to other professionals who can provide specialized expertise or services to support business growth.

9. HUMAN RESOURCES AND RECRUITING

HR professionals and recruiters may refer candidates to other professionals or businesses within their network for job opportunities or specialized services.

10. MARKETING AND PUBLIC RELATIONS

Marketing and PR professionals often collaborate with graphic designers, content creators, and web developers, making referrals within their network to provide comprehensive solutions to clients.

11. EDUCATION AND TRAINING

Professionals in the education and training industry may refer students or clients to other educators, trainers, or institutions offering complementary programs or services.

12. NONPROFIT AND PHILANTHROPY

Individuals involved in nonprofits or philanthropic organizations often refer supporters, donors, or volunteers to other organizations that align with their mission.

13. NETWORKING GROUPS AND ASSOCIATIONS

Professionals who actively participate in industry-specific networking groups, associations, or chambers of commerce are likely to make referrals within their community.

Do not skip this homework!

This key relationships list will continue to get refined and narrowed down as you learn more about each component of the Infinite Referral Advantage®. Then, in chapter 11, I'll explain how you can continue to maintain, cultivate, and refine your list along with my favorite strategy for staying consistent.

When you lean into your strengths as a local small business owner, you don't just beat Goliath at his game, you change the game entirely. In the pages that follow, you'll learn more about each of these relationships and the low-cost, low-commitment, and high-impact ways you can develop value-driven relationships that last and build your own Infinite Referral Advantage®.

CHAPTER 6

THE INCOME ADVANTAGE: SMALL BUSINESS OWNERS

REFERRALS DONE RIGHT

Remember Gina, our overwhelmed small business owner from chapter 2? She spent many late nights scouring the internet for a quick fix to her financial woes. All she found was more ways to spend money she didn't have, only to learn new versions of the same kind of traditional marketing that got her in trouble in the first place.

She wasn't a Goliath, and she had real-time evidence that those tactics created an ever-growing chasm between the life she imagined for her family and the one where she was up to her eyeballs in debt.

Feeling frustrated and in need of a little caffeinated pick-me-up from all her late-night searching, she headed out to her local coffee shop and found a few familiar faces. Seated around a small table in the corner were a local realtor, a mortgage broker, and an attorney, who had all stopped by and introduced themselves at her storefront over the past few weeks. She immediately remembered their open invitation to join them every Monday morning and smiled as they waved and motioned to the empty chair at their table.

After she got her latte, Gina was happy to join them, and they spent the hour getting to know each other better. She learned that her son was in the same preschool as the realtor's and that the mortgage broker liked lattes better than any kind of coffee, just like she did. She found out that the attorney recently inherited his law firm and is trying to figure out how to run a small business for the first time. The connection with others to whom she could relate felt amazing to her.

As they got up to go back to their home away from home up and down Main Street, Gina promised she'd be back to join them the next week. This Monday morning caffeine club was for these small business owners to gather for venting, support, and learning about each other as people.

THE INCOME ADVANTAGE: SMALL BUSINESS OWNERS

After some time, Gina received a call from prospective clients who just bought a new house with the help of her realtor friend. He referred the new homeowners to her for insurance. When they asked her if she knew a good attorney in the area, she referred them to her other Monday coffee friend.

And just like that, this little army of Davids realized that the relationships they formed were not only fulfilling but could also lead to sharing their services among clients in a more meaningful way.

Small business owners are the unsung heroes of a community. They bring character and uniqueness to the local landscape. Local entrepreneurs often reflect the community's identity, offering personalized goods and services that cater to the specific needs and preferences of the residents.

Economically, they contribute significantly by creating jobs and donating to local sports teams, clubs, events, and activities. This, in turn, helps with wealth distribution within the community, strengthening its economic foundation. Small business owners also tend to purchase their goods and services locally, creating a cycle of support that benefits everyone.

For many of us, this is why we started our business—we are local people serving local people. Overall, small businesses contribute to the social, cultural, and economic fabric of a community, making them vital contributors to its well-being. I could make a strong case that the health of a community is directly tied to the number of strong small businesses within it. It only makes sense to find ways to work together with other small business owners.

WHY DON'T YOU KNOW MORE SBOS?

My advice here sounds so simple: build relationships with the other small business owners in your area. Team up over time to help your community work with the best people your town has to offer, and you'll see long-term success. If it's that easy, why aren't more people creating these SBO-to-SBO relationships all the time?

Well, I don't believe anyone dreams of starting a small business just to isolate themselves and disconnect from every other small business owner in their community. But it happens. We get so focused on what we are building that sometimes days turn into weeks and months into years and we lose touch with those around us doing that. Other times we know we need to be out among other people in our local connection economy, but the interactions feel silted, forced, and transactional.

We also tend to overthink and overcomplicate things.

Maybe you don't feel like it's worth your time to go out and "make new friends" when you have so much you already need to do in a day. While I agree that your day-to-day operations deserve your full attention, you and I both know there are at least ten minutes of your day that could be better spent making a meaningful connection with a fellow SBO.

Perhaps you fear the unknown. Maybe you've been doing this for a while now, and you're comfortable with what's working. You don't see a need to change things just because I'm here telling you to. Stepping out of your comfort zone can be challenging. However, as SBOs, we have to force ourselves to become comfortable with discomfort or we can become complacent. When a small business owner becomes complacent, there isn't room for growth.

It may feel like you'll lose customers if you refer them to other people. I understand this one, and I lived this early on in my career. But once I shifted my focus away from what the competition was doing and went all in on the tremendous value we offered, everything changed. Once you fully understand your worth, you'll act in accordance with confidence. And that's when you understand you are your only competition.

It could also be that you have tried to connect in the past and it gives you a headache just thinking about it. But if I had a dollar for every time an SBO said, "I already tried that, Scott, and it didn't work," I'd have bushels and bushels of dollars!

> **Once you fully understand your worth, you'll act in accordance with confidence.**

For you, I say, it's time to remember that failure is a form of feedback. We never actually lose if we learn from the experience. Use what you learned and set clear expectations when you start talking about the next collaboration.

YOU'RE MISSING OUT

When you choose not to connect with other SBOs, you can miss out on so many different kinds of opportunities that you simply cannot do on your own. Building relationships with other SBOs can create a strong referral network—the most powerful, cost-effective marketing tool! But if you don't put yourself out there, you can't connect people to potential customers, and those SBOs can't refer people to you either.

Neglecting relationships with other small businesses can have several consequences in the broader context of marketing. Here are some potential repercussions:

- You're missing out on potential referral opportunities. When businesses have strong connections, they are more likely to refer customers to each other, expanding each other's customer base.
- You limit the reach of your marketing efforts. You may not benefit from exposure to other customer bases when you aren't willing to cross-promote.
- You're missing out on the opportunity to jointly organize events, promotions, or marketing campaigns that could amplify your brand presence.
- You're reducing your visibility and influence in the local business community by remaining isolated.
- You're weakening your online presence when you don't connect with other SBOs on social media, leaving opportunities for viability through organic "cross-pollination" out of your reach.

I can make this list a whole lot longer, but I think you get the picture.

> But, Scott, I have a small business, and I go out of my way to support other small businesses. They don't always reciprocate. Why should I keep trying?

To you, I say, it's commendable that you actively support other small businesses, and it's understandable to feel disappointed if the reciprocity isn't always evident. But let's consider a few reasons why you may want to continue your efforts.

THE INCOME ADVANTAGE: SMALL BUSINESS OWNERS

Building relationships takes time. Remember, a tremendous amount of success is awarded to the people who continuously show up. The entire Infinite Referral Advantage® is about *playing the long game*. I recognize and acknowledge there are quicker and easier ways to create short-term wins. However, those avenues are typically more expensive and more short-lived.

While some businesses may not reciprocate immediately, they may remember your support in the long run. Consistent efforts can lead to stronger, more mutually beneficial relationships over time. The focus is not one immediate introduction but rather hundreds of introductions for years to come.

Your commitment to supporting other businesses reflects positively on your own brand. Customers and other businesses in the community may appreciate and remember your efforts, enhancing your reputation. Also, if your intent is genuine, you'll have no concerns regarding immediate reciprocity.

Actively supporting other businesses contributes to the overall health of the local business community. As more businesses engage in collaborative efforts, it creates a supportive ecosystem that benefits everyone. Collaboration often opens doors to unexpected opportunities. Even if the direct reciprocation is not immediate, your efforts may lead to new connections, partnerships, or business opportunities down the line.

Your commitment to supporting others sets an example for other businesses in the community. It demonstrates leadership and a willingness to contribute to the collective success of small businesses. Strength and leadership will improve your personal brand. Businesses that share similar values are more likely to collaborate over time.

If you align yourself with businesses that share your values, the likelihood of reciprocal support increases. You are supporting this SBO because you trust and respect them. *Trust* and *respect* aren't words to be taken lightly. They take time. When you stop supporting an SBO that you trust and respect because they don't immediately reciprocate, then why would they trust and respect you?

Supporting other businesses contributes to a thriving local economy. A healthy business environment benefits everyone, including your own business, in the long run. While immediate reciprocation is desired, it's not likely—and that's okay. The long-term benefits of building a collaborative and supportive business community will outweigh the short-term frustrations.

Keep nurturing those connections, and you'll find that your efforts contribute to a more vibrant and interconnected business landscape. The successful business you desire will be built on mutual trust and respect from fellow SBOs and people in your community. This happens over time, not by constantly quitting on relationships that don't bear immediate fruit.

COLLABORATION MYTHS TO BUST

A well-structured collaboration between small businesses ensures that all parties gain value in some way. It's about finding a fair and mutually beneficial arrangement. When doing your best to serve your intended market is the primary focus, it's a win for everyone involved.

Debunking some of the most common myths about collaboration can open up new possibilities and build stronger, more resilient relationships among yourselves. Let's get to the myth busting:

Myth: Collaboration is only for big businesses.
Reality: Small businesses can benefit greatly from working together, pooling resources, and tapping into each other's strengths.

Myth: Collaboration is a sign of weakness or inability to compete.
Reality: Collaborating can enhance competitiveness by combining skills, resources, and networks, ultimately benefiting all parties involved. SBOs need to check their egos at the door and shift to an abundance mindset when it comes to collaborative efforts. There is plenty of business for everyone and even more for those who realize the value of joining forces to create win-win situations.

Myth: Collaboration is always time-consuming and complicated.
Reality: While collaboration requires effort, it doesn't always have to be complicated. Simple, targeted collaborations can be effective without overwhelming resources. The key here is to start small and build. Too often, owners try to accomplish everything all at once. It's crucial to think long-term, have attainable goals, get things on the calendar, and understand that it will often take many months to gain traction.

Myth: Collaboration only happens within the same industry.
Reality: Businesses from different industries can bring fresh perspectives and ideas, leading to innovative

solutions. Almost all the SBOs I collaborate with are from parallel industries (people who offer different products and services to the same people I want to work with).

Myth: All collaborators must have identical goals.
Reality: While shared goals can be beneficial, collaborators can also have complementary goals. Diverse objectives can lead to a more well-rounded and versatile collaboration. It's important to remain realistic. Too often, people desire significant results immediately. If anything were that easy, everyone would already know about it and be doing it. All good things take time, especially in the relationship marketing space.

Myth: Collaboration is only about cost-cutting.
Reality: Collaboration can bring about mutual growth and increased revenue, not just cost savings. It's a strategic move to create new opportunities and expand market reach. I view collaboration as value added for the customer first, an opportunity to increase brand awareness in a new market second, and doing both on a limited budget as the cherry on top.

Myth: Collaborating means giving up control.
Reality: It doesn't necessarily mean giving up control but rather sharing responsibilities and decision-making for mutual benefit. Again, egos must be checked at the door, and clearly defined goals regarding what the target market will receive from these efforts must be the focus.

Myth: Collaboration is a one-time effort.
Reality: Successful collaboration often requires ongoing communication and adaptation. It's a dynamic process that may evolve over time. One-time efforts and events will provide false feelings of failure.

Myth: Collaborating means sacrificing individual identity.
Reality: The unique strengths of each small business owner can contribute to the success of the collaboration. Top-of-mind awareness is created by people seeing and hearing your name, image, or logo as often as possible. So long as you work to create a strong personal brand, collaboration only improves individual identities.

When creating connections and collaborating with other small business owners, the process is to plant, *cultivate,* and then harvest. The first few efforts are simply planting seeds. The magic is in the ongoing cultivation process. Where SBOs get tripped up is planting and then instantly expecting an immediate, bountiful harvest. When that doesn't happen, they deem the efforts a failure and move on. The reality is that you need to allow some time for the roots to grow, and then the seeds will sprout when they're ready—no need to douse them in Miracle-Gro!

The process of creating and strengthening relationships is like gardening: you plant, cultivate, and harvest. Being a part of service organizations, networking with others, and giving back to the community is all about planting the seeds. Doing all this consistently—adding value and helping others—is the cultivation process. After the seeds (relationships) have been cultivated long enough, you'll be ready to harvest (gain new opportunities).

POSITIVE RELATIONSHIPS MAKE NATURAL REFERRALS

Think about the people you recommend and introduce to your friends and family. In fact, narrow it down to just one person or business. Why do you feel so strongly about sharing them with the people you love the most in the world?

Is it because they run numerous television ads? Or maybe they're visible on multiple billboards along highways? Or perhaps their Google ad spend on targeted behavioral marketing is second to none?

No? None of those are the reasons you introduce that person in your head to friends and family. *Of course not.*

My guess is, it's because you've personally gotten to know them. You don't just *think* they are a good person who is great at what they do; you've seen it with your own eyes over the years.

Anyone who mentions needing payroll services to me is going to get a full-blown, enthusiastic endorsement for my payroll guy, Frank, and his team. Frank could start charging me double the rate I'm paying now, and I'd still gladly pay it. (Hopefully, he's not reading this.)

Why?

Because he has taken the time to understand me and my business. But he didn't stop there. He's also invested time to get to know my family. He proactively reaches out to me and is consistent with follow-ups. He engages with my social media content and promotes everything I do. Frank sends birthday cards and gives thoughtful gifts. He introduces his clients, friends, and family to me. He supports charitable and community events I'm involved with. And he even showed up at my father's funeral.

Why?

Because Frank is an A+ human who truly cares. Yes, he's knowledgeable and professional when it comes to payroll services, but so are dozens of others I could work with. I remain loyal to Frank and his team because he operates with a servant's heart and has mastered the art of relationship marketing.

When small business owners go out of their way to support and connect with each other, incredible connections are formed. Those connections ripple out. And the more SBOs connect, the more people they can serve in meaningful ways.

Have you heard of The Farmers Market Coalition? If not, you should check it out. This organization supports and promotes farmers' markets across the United States. By fostering relationships between local farmers, vendors, and the community, they have significantly boosted the success of individual markets. The emphasis on community engagement, personal connections, and shared values has not only increased the popularity of farmers' markets but also supported local economies and created a sense of community belonging.

When was the last time you visited your local coffee shop or café? Think about it—they thrive on relationship marketing within their communities. They often become social hubs, fostering a sense of belonging for everyone who passes through their door. By knowing their regular customers, engaging in community events, and supporting local initiatives, these businesses create a loyal customer base. People choose these establishments not just for the coffee but for the community atmosphere they provide.

COMMIT TO CONSISTENCY

If you want different results for your small business, it's time to take on a different perspective. In order to see the benefits of these relationships, you have to shift your thoughts away from, *Scott, this sounds interesting,* to *Hey, I'm committed to doing this.* You may have heard about the difference between *committed* and *interested,* but let's refresh your memory.

If you feel interested in something, you have a sense of curiosity about the topic. It's enough to make you want to casually check something out. But as challenges arrive or other interesting things shine a little brighter, it's easy to walk away.

But if you are committed to something, it's more than the initial curiosity. It drives you to focus more intensely. You create a more sustainable level of involvement, and that keeps you consistent even when challenges appear.

The Infinite Referral Advantage˚ is built inside the heart of small business owners who are committed to consistency. And no, I don't mean this is a New Year's resolution kind of thing. It's about staying the course by demonstrating dedication, persistence, and a willingness to go the extra mile for someone else.

Anyone can do something once in a while, but consistency is key in relationship building. While the Goliaths are trying to build relationships from afar, you have the advantage of letting other small business owners get to know *you*. This makes all the difference. So why is consistency important?

When people see a small business owner consistently delivering on promises, they develop a sense of trust and reliability. Trust is a crucial factor in building and maintaining relationships.

Every time you show up as yourself, you solidify what you stand for and the values you represent.

As other small business owners learn what to expect from you in terms of quality, messaging, and customer experience, they are more likely to introduce people to you. It shows that you are serious, professional, and dedicated to delivering a consistent level of quality, which enhances your credibility in the eyes of referral partners.

Small business owners who have positive and consistent experiences with you or your brand are more likely to become loyal advocates who continue to choose to recommend you over competitors.

CONNECT CANDIDLY

This next part might sound a little crazy, but I'm asking you to find ways that you can genuinely support other small business owners without expecting anything in return. When Becky Smith showed up the first time, she left an incredible impression. She took the time to learn more about me and gave me the opportunity to get to know her. There was no sense of urgency. She didn't run in, toss her business card at me, and rush out to her next appointment. But she did let me know about her role in the community and then offered ways she could help me connect with other people. Her mission was to serve and connect SBOs. A few months later, I knew who I could refer a customer to with confidence.

When you consider ways of initiating new relationships with other small business owners, always stay true to your authentic self. It's great to see what works for others, but when you take the time to consider ways you enjoy supporting others, you'll give yourself the opportunity to have fun while you build genuine relationships.

Think of building these relationships as a "choose your own adventure" journey rather than a "color by number" situation. You started your own business because you have something unique to share with the world. If you wanted to be told what to do and how to do it, you would have applied for a job instead.

When I work with individuals, we begin by creating a system of meaningful contacts—one every four weeks. At each point of contact, we consider multiple ways to communicate, so you can choose what makes the most sense for who you are. Maybe you like a more casual setting, so you pop in, introduce yourself, and invite the other SBO to grab some coffee. It could be a simple Follow on their social media account or a handwritten note letting them know you wanted to see if they'd like to connect.

However you choose, it's imperative that your goal remains the same: you're there to see how you can help support their business by creating a lasting business relationship. Over time you'll see the natural progression of the relationship turn into opportunities for collaboration, networking, and yes, even referrals.

CONSISTENTLY COLLABORATE, CONTEMPLATE, AND CULTIVATE

Measuring the success of relationship-building involves assessing both quantitative and qualitative indicators. One tangible way for you to gauge the effectiveness of your efforts is customer retention rates. Ask yourself, *Are the new customers sticking with me? Are they repeat customers?*

Measure the percentage of customers who continue to do business with your company over time. A high customer retention rate indicates the success of relationship marketing in fostering loyalty. Typically, traditional marketing will offer spikes in interest based on a one-time deal or special offer. Then they will jump to another company once they offer a new deal. (If they buy from you on price, they'll leave you for a better price.) In contrast, customers who are introduced to you via personal relationships and realize your value are more loyal. Calculate the CLV (customer lifetime value) to understand the total revenue generated by a customer over their entire relationship with your business. A rising CLV signifies successful relationship building.

Monitor the number of referrals generated from fellow SBOs. High referral rates indicate that peers are not only finding value in your relationship but also actively promoting your business to others.

Analyze conversion rates at different stages of the customer journey. Improved conversion rates, especially in customer acquisition and retention efforts, suggest that relationship marketing strategies are resonating with the audience. Introductions (or referrals) will come to you with baseline trust already established. Because of this, you'll notice a significantly higher conversion rate from referrals compared to traditional marketing efforts.

Gather feedback through surveys or direct customer interactions. Positive feedback, testimonials, and insights into customer satisfaction provide qualitative evidence of relationship marketing success.

Monitor engagement metrics on social media platforms. Increased likes, shares, comments, 5-star reviews, and positive sentiment on social channels suggest that your audience is actively engaging with your brand.

Evaluate the growth and engagement within any online or offline communities you've built. A thriving community is a qualitative sign that your relationship marketing efforts are fostering a sense of belonging and connection.

Measure the success of personalized interactions. If referral partners respond positively to personalized messages or gifts, it indicates that your efforts to tailor experiences are resonating.

Encourage and showcase customer stories and testimonials. Positive narratives from customers about their experiences with your business are powerful indicators of relationship-marketing success.

Assess the outcomes of collaborations and partnerships with other businesses. Successful collaborations can lead to shared success, increased visibility, and positive brand associations.

By combining quantitative metrics with qualitative indicators, you can gain a comprehensive understanding of the impact of your relationship marketing strategies. Regularly reviewing these metrics allows for ongoing refinement and optimization of your relationship-building efforts.

ALWAYS KEEP AN OPEN MIND

Listening actively demonstrates your commitment to understanding and addressing their concerns. Clearly communicate your intentions and values. Be transparent about your goals and how a collaboration can be mutually beneficial. Address any misconceptions or suspicions directly to build trust.

To improve the quality of your relationships, increase the quantity of questions you ask. Listen closely to the answers you hear, and work to find common ground that aligns with the interests and values you both have. Emphasize the potential benefits and positive outcomes that can result from a collaborative relationship. Never lose sight of what's in it for them. Suggest things starting with small thoughts, ideas, or collaborations. This allows them to test the waters, build trust gradually, and assess the compatibility of working together.

Work collaboratively to find solutions or compromises that address concerns and create a more conducive environment for collaboration. Flexibility and a willingness to adapt can be crucial in overcoming initial suspicions.

Remember, building meaningful connections with fellow SBOs is an ongoing process. Patience, empathy, and a genuine commitment to understanding their struggles and providing solutions are at the core of strong and enduring relationships.

TODAY'S HOMEWORK

- ✔ Go back to your key relationships list from chapter 5.
- ✔ Highlight the names of small business owners in your area that you could invite for coffee or lunch.
    - ○ They don't all have to be in the same industry, just in and around your community.
- ✔ Choose one person from your list.
- ✔ Decide if you'd rather send a note, a DM, or stop by, then go ahead and invite them.
- ✔ Once you have a coffee or lunch date, brainstorm some ways you could help them that you'd enjoy doing.

- ✔ During your conversation, begin by just getting to know each other as people.
- ✔ If it makes sense throughout your conversation, ask them if there is a way you could help. If it doesn't naturally come up, save your ideas for another day.
- ✔ Don't trust your memory! It will fail you at some point.
  - ○ Shortly after any conversations you have with people from your key relationships list from this day on, jot down things that are important to remember. Trust me, you're too busy to keep everything in your brain for the next time you meet up. This way you can refresh your memory without having to ask them the same questions over and over.

CHAPTER 7

THE IMPACT ADVANTAGE: SCHOOLS

I wanted to write a book aimed at teens, offering insights into life's real-world challenges that are often not learned in school. However, I hadn't been a teenager in thirty years, and I questioned if I had an adequate understanding of today's teens.

I needed help. A family member taught at a local high school, so I called in a favor.

"How many students do you teach?"

"One hundred and three," she replied. "Why?"

"I've created an anonymous five-question survey to gain some insights from teenagers," I told her. "Would you be willing to give your students the questionnaire for me?"

My relative agreed that I could survey her high schoolers. Now, mind you, these were primarily sixteen-year-old students, one year away from completing high school and living in an above-average community based on socioeconomic data.

I asked these students: "What self-beliefs are holding you back?"

Of the 103 responses, 88 involved language of negative self-perception or fear.

Here are a few examples, cut-and-pasted verbatim from the survey:

- "Mentally, I may not be stable enough to be as successful as I want."
- "I have doubts about my future."
- "I have fears of failing."
- "My lack of belief in myself."
- "My belief that I won't be good enough."
- "Beliefs of self-doubt and being very hard on myself have definitely taken a toll and held me back."
- "I'm not good enough, or that I'm afraid to fail."
- "That I'm not good enough."
- "Everything, including myself, has to be perfect."

Reading their words was heartbreaking yet illuminating. It shed light on a pressing issue in today's kids: a crisis of confidence among our youth.

Connecting the dots, I realized these struggles extended beyond adolescence. Adults I coached in my consulting business were almost twice, or even three times, these kids' ages, and they echo similar sentiments when I ask them questions like "What's holding you back?" Their answers are "I lack confidence"; "I'm scared to fail"; "I'm not good enough"; "I'm not prepared"; or "If I try, I'll fail."

These folks didn't devise their self-conceptions in isolation; they were influenced by external forces. What you are told about yourself becomes ingrained, shaping your identity. As a result, most adults carry the same insecurities they had as teens because they were never taught to challenge these beliefs. They internalized their doubts, causing stress, complacency, and frustration. Even worse, some adults reach the point of resignation. I can't tell you how often people in their forties and fifties say to me, "Scott, it doesn't matter; it's too late for me now."

But what if these people had a mentor or a community leader during their teen years who had told them that self-doubt is natural? What if they'd said it's okay to have those feelings but the key to success lies in not believing them? Imagine if someone had shared their own struggles and failures and offered hope and guidance. What if just one student took these lessons to heart, transformed their lack of belief into unwavering confidence, and went on to achieve incredible results that positively impacted millions? I had the opportunity to share my thoughts in a TEDx Talk titled "Silence That Voice" on April 11, 2024.

Check out my "Silence That Voice" TEDx Talk at: scottgrates.com

Check out my "Silence That Voice" TEDx Talk at: scottgrates.com

As small business owners, we intimately know failure, challenge, and success in a way many others don't. We can be that adult who fosters that impact. That's what prompted me to write *Essential F-Words for Teens* and is the why behind my efforts to establish relationships with schools in my community.

Schools are the backbone of every community, and part of the beauty of working with schools is that you hit the Reset button each year. All the opportunities from the previous year are new again. If you worked with the senior class, you have a whole new class of seniors this year. If you worked with the Future Business Leaders of America club, you now have new members to work with. The long-term opportunities and benefits of schools are second to none.

Now that I have relationships established with local schools, they often contact me for seminars, workshops, and even keynote speeches at commencement ceremonies. I sponsor certain events annually and offer prizes to elementary classrooms for being a "bucket filler" (spreading positivity). My business recognizes a teacher and student of the month, and I give scholarships to graduating seniors. Our agency also offers job-shadowing opportunities and summer internships, help in building résumés, and mock interviews to prepare students for the real world.

All this creates positive social media content and a buzz throughout the community and connects me on deeper levels with customers, future customers, and potential employees.

SCHOOLS AS INFINITE REFERRAL PIPELINES

It's not uncommon for small business owners to engage with schools when they want to do good things and help people. The problem is that we often take the easy route, thinking that writing a check to the basketball team is enough. It's not.

You can purchase a gym membership, but you won't get stronger if you never walk through the doors. You can buy healthy food, but you won't be better nourished if you never eat it. You can write a check to sponsor a team or event, but if you just stop there, it won't have the impact you desire.

Like other key relationships, schools take time to pay off. That's okay. And the honest statement is that you may not know if your efforts in schools lead to new business. (Unless they specifically tell you, if you're using traditional ROI metrics, you may be attributing actual school-inspired clients to other marketing initiatives.)

The key to leveraging your investment in schools is to adjust your approach to school-based relationships.

The key to leveraging your investment in schools is to adjust your approach to school-based relationships. The issue isn't that schools are a waste of time for business development or bottomless pits for altruism. The problem is that we often choose the path of least resistance, thinking that simply checking a box marked "school" will help you create your Infinite Referral Advantage˚, and it won't.

I also want to add that if you don't want to work with kids yourself, that's absolutely fine. You can't wear all the hats in your business or outreach, nor should you. You can delegate the job to somebody on your team who does. Do what you enjoy most, the things that bring you the most joy, and that you're good at. Forcing yourself into roles and situations that don't light you up will negatively impact you and your business. Just make sure you are delegating, not ignoring, the things you don't like.

Do you know who else is skipping school as part of their marketing plan? Your competition! Schools are one of the least-crowded spaces in your community. Working closely with schools is a space you can easily own (unless someone else reading this book acts faster than you).

HOW TO MEASURE THE ROI ON VALUE-BASED SCHOOL CONNECTIONS

To develop your Infinite Referral Advantage® with schools, you are playing a very, very long game. That's okay. There is marketing that will help today, and then there are future-generation marketing efforts that tomorrow you'll be glad you did. Schools are the latter. Investing in them is future-proofing your business.

Playing the long game isn't bad. When acquiring a fifty-year-old customer today, your best-case scenario is twenty years of potential business. However, when you acquire a twenty-year-old customer a few years from now, they have the long-term potential to be a loyal customer for fifty years.

Hundreds of my customers today once sat in an audience during a career day, teen driver safety event, financial literacy workshop, or even assemblies where I brought in external paid speakers into the school.

Many of my customers initially allowed me to serve them because they saw how active and influential I was with their children. Without prompting, these parents created posts highlighting my efforts and shared my agency's posts with their followers.

Besides these futuristic goals however, you can also measure the ROI on value-based school connections in several ways.

Quantitative Metrics

- **Volunteer Hours**: Track the total number of volunteer hours you and your employees contribute. This can be a straightforward metric indicating the level of commitment and engagement.
- **Number of Volunteers**: Measure the number of employees participating in school events. This metric reflects the scale of involvement and can be compared across different events.
- **Event Attendance**: If the volunteerism involves organizing or supporting events, track the attendance figures. Higher attendance may indicate increased community engagement.

Student Impact Metrics

- **Student Attendance**: Monitor changes in student attendance on days when business volunteers are present. Increased attendance could be a positive outcome of the engagement.
- **Academic Performance**: If feasible, collaborate with the school to track changes in academic performance among students who have been recipients of volunteer-led initiatives or programs.

Feedback and Surveys

- **Employee Satisfaction**: Gather feedback from participating employees through surveys. Ask about their experiences, the impact they feel they've made, and their overall satisfaction with the volunteer opportunities.

- **School Staff Feedback**: Collect feedback from school staff regarding the impact of business volunteers on school events. This can provide insights into the perceived benefits and areas for improvement.

Community Engagement

- **Community Outreach Metrics**: Measure the reach and impact of community events organized or supported by business volunteers. You could include the number of attendees, media coverage, or social media engagement.
- **Partnership Growth**: Assess whether your collaboration has led to increased community partnerships, demonstrating a positive impact on the broader community.

Success Stories and Testimonials

- **Compile Stories**: Collect success stories and testimonials from employees and the school community. These anecdotes can provide qualitative evidence of the meaningful impact of volunteerism.

Employee Retention and Satisfaction

- **Retention Rates**: Assess whether employees who actively participate in volunteer programs have higher retention rates. Increased employee retention can be an indirect measure of the success and satisfaction derived from volunteerism.

Nurturing a critical relationship with somebody in the business field may yield new introductions, expand your brand's reach, or create an extraordinary collaboration. However, making a positive impact on the life of one child could change the future. Your legacy is determined not by what you accomplished but by those you impacted.

A SOLUTION FOR THE SBO WHO DOESN'T KNOW WHERE OR HOW TO START

All right, so you're on board with the idea that schools are another smooth stone in your slingshot and an important part of building your Infinite Referral Advantage˚. But where do you start? What's step one to adopting the Infinite Referral Advantage˚ at school?

You don't have to do anything overwhelming—in fact, you shouldn't. Start small. Anything beyond writing a check will get you going. For instance, you could speak to a high school class or participate in career day. You can offer to meet one-on-one with juniors or seniors who express an interest in your field. One of my favorite simple activities is sponsoring the "Bucket Filler Award." Teachers select students who are "filling up other people's buckets with encouragement," and I provide and present the prizes. Ask a friend or family member who teaches how you can help them. Call your local school, the one your kids go to, or the one you graduated from, and talk to the administrators and ask what they need and how you can get involved and support their work.

Once you've gotten your feet wet with schools, I can almost guarantee you'll want to wade in deeper. And really, there's no end to what you can do in a school environment. When I ran low on ideas, I borrowed some from three other agency owners I know: Alice, Martin, and Kanecia. You may want to as well.

Alice does an annual *Shark Tank*–type event where students develop business ideas, build a plan, and present it to Alice and the other "sharks" she's recruited. This falls under both schools and fellow SBO collaboration as she invites these people in her network to join her as she serves.

Martin partners with a school to present an "Unsung Hero Award" each year. Teachers at each grade level select one student who demonstrates kindness and goodwill toward others when nobody else is looking. Often these are the type of student who doesn't consistently get recognized for academic or athletic achievement. Then, at the end of the school year, Martin charters a bus and purchases group tickets to a major league baseball game. Each winning student can bring two people to the game. It's a "home run" throughout the year and creates excellent social media content.

Kanecia takes her involvement with schools to the next level by organizing a prom for special-needs students. She goes all out—fundraises to secure the facility, decorates, provides music, and even arranges attire for students who need it. While this idea falls into the school's side of the Infinite Referral Advantage®, Kanecia's fundraising and promotion for the event also involves fellow SBOs, service organizations, some star customers, and social media.

In my town, I led a fun initiative called the Kindness Rocks Project with seventy elementary school students involved with the Kiwanis K-Kids club. They painted hundreds of rocks and wrote inspirational messages on them like: "You matter"; "You rock"; "You're amazing"; "Smile"; and "Be happy." Then they found places around the community to leave them. This way someone else would find the rock with the kind message, improving their day.

Each student crafted five messages on five different rocks, totaling 350 rocks in all. That's potentially at least 350 smiles and happy stories from people around the community who found them. This initiative not only spreads joy but also

- → fostered collaboration with a local civic group and teachers,
- → helped 70 students realize the power of intentional acts of kindness, and
- → made at least 350 happier people in the community.

Consider reaching out to your local Kiwanis International chapter. Their mission is to serve the youth in the community, and they offer established programs with schools like K-Kids (grades 3–5), Builders Club (grades 6–8), Key Club (grades 9–12), and Circle K (college students). Also, check with nearby Rotary Clubs and Chambers of Commerce chapters to find out what programs they sponsor.

Don't overlook organizations that are unique to your community. In my area, The Genesis Group began in 2000 to bring together business and community leaders to promote regional economic, social, and cultural interests. This organization holds multiple events with schools each year, and they're always looking for business owners to volunteer.

Government entities like New York's Board of Cooperative Educational Services (BOCES) can also be valuable partners. Established by the New York legislature, BOCES provides shared educational programs and services to school districts. Many of the programs and initiatives that would interest SBOs are structured (and often funded) by BOCES. Check your state's Department of Education website to learn if they have their own version of this service.

In addition, consider implementing your own programs tailored to benefit students. You can use mine, Career After Classroom® (careerafterclassroom.com), which is a six-week real-world mindset certificate program where students spend approximately fifteen minutes daily with content designed to benefit them regardless of their future career path. Or you can design your own curriculum to suit your specific needs.

As the program concludes, students will have delved into ten hours of life-changing content and received a personal playbook—a how-to guide on building a résumé, standing out during interviews, and getting launched with community service and networking. We allow other small business owners to purchase bundles of these programs for schools, clubs, or even their teenage customers.

When you invest in the program, your business also receives ready-made public relations guides, press release templates, and social media posts along with your purchase. This enables you to offer this six-week certificate program at no cost to students and simultaneously receive positive relationship-marketing benefits.

Schools are great at teaching students academic skills, but we can teach them real-world life lessons as business owners and community leaders. For example, many kids believe failing makes them a failure. Yet as adults and small business owners, we understand firsthand that failure serves as valuable feedback. Show me a successful professional in any field, and I'll show you somebody who has experienced countless failures and learned from them.

Children are impressionable and tend to remember those who invest time in them. Sometimes they pay more attention to those of us who come in from the outside world than their teachers. Our words matter, and our messages resonate with them on a deeper level.

I'm approaching fifty years old, and I still vividly remember a local radio DJ visiting my fourth-grade classroom. He had cool clothes and long hair. In my mind, he was Jon Bon Jovi! This man shared a behind-the-scenes glimpse into how things worked at the radio station so we could hear our favorite songs at home.

For the next year of my life, I played cassette tapes and talked to my make-believe audience (using a cool radio voice) between songs. Then as that song played, I feverishly scrambled to figure out what the next song to play would be. That DJ pulled back the curtain and showed me that I could do what he did, and suddenly I wanted to. I believe I could if I worked at it. Also, what radio station did I listen to (and forced my parents to) for the remainder of my childhood? Yup, *his* station . . . 96.9 on your dial, the rock of Central New York, WOUR.

He made a lasting impression on me and picked up loyal listeners (customers) along the way.

Another win-win.

NAVIGATING THE CHALLENGES

As local small business owners, we align closely with the objectives and goals of schools, including community development, workforce preparation, local economy improvement, and the neighborhood's overall well-being. While schools play a fantastic role in offering a wide variety of general subject areas, they can't dive deeply into how that knowledge will become valuable to students in various industries. That's where our partnerships become indispensable.

Through involvement and initiatives like internships, mentorships, or joint community service projects, small business owners can demonstrate to students firsthand why their education matters and how they can and will apply that knowledge in practical settings.

Unfortunately, volunteerism is at an all-time low. However, this trend creates a fantastic opportunity for those of us willing and able to step up and help. If you want a school or local civic organization to say *yes* to you, simply offer your time to support them. You won't be disappointed.

When meeting with school administrators, your focus should stay on them, as it should with any other connection you want to make. You are leading with your servant's heart and offering your time and money to help move the school and each student closer to their goals and expectations for the year.

Speaking at career days or teen driver safety days, volunteering at fundraisers, offering financial literacy workshops, spending time at events, or mentoring specific clubs are all meaningful ways to get involved. Whenever I speak at a school event, I try to make a lasting impression, and I make sure to send students home with something branded they can keep or share with the adults in their lives.

I meet with district superintendents and principals at numerous local schools each year. My message is simple: "I'm here to help." I was once a confused but optimistic student myself. I lacked self-confidence and needed mentors to help guide me. More than anything, I needed to see what opportunities were available and figure out what I enjoyed and didn't. Today I am eager to be that mentor that I once needed. I'm excited to share lessons from the real world with students who are seeking guidance and want to explore various opportunities.

During these meetings, I pose many open-ended questions to administrators, aiming to understand their goals and initiatives.

Then I offer my support to the district however they see fit. While not every school I meet with has taken me up on my offer, most do, and an overwhelming number of opportunities are sent my way each school year.

When talking with school leaders, it's crucial to establish clear collaboration objectives. Whether it's improving educational outcomes, enhancing community engagement, or fostering skill development, it all begins with having well-defined goals to measure success.

I also prioritize the number of students impacted by an initiative. For example, if two hundred students hear me speak on a career day, then two hundred students will leave with at least one takeaway. This allows me to demonstrate the tangible impact of my efforts to the community, my customers, and my audience on social media. One hour can positively impact two hundred students today.

Moreover, beyond audience size, true results come from student feedback. Following a career day presentation, you can solicit student feedback on what they learned, how it impacted them, and what they plan to do with this new knowledge. This data and testimonials enable me to tailor future engagements to their needs as well.

In terms of frequency, I recommend engaging with schools at least once a month. We will dive deeper into this in chapter 11. There I will show you how you can create an annual calendar of events with the school before each year begins and will also help keep you on task.

Your activities don't have to be complicated to be effective. Simply sponsoring a student or teacher of the month or partnering with an individual classroom or grade level on incentive programs like my "Bucket Filler Award," which I talked about earlier. The winning student can receive a coupon for free ice cream or perhaps a pizza certificate (from a local small business you can collaborate with to further maximize your advantage).

It can even just be giving every kid a book. After I released *Essential F-Words for Teens*, I received an email from Melissa, an insurance agency owner I'd never met. She had purchased 150 copies of the book (thank you, Melissa!) so she could gift one to every graduating senior in her town. The school invited Melissa to speak during a special assembly in their auditorium. During her talk, she shared her favorite takeaways from the book, personal stories from her entrepreneurial journey, and encouraging messages of hope.

A local television station caught wind of this and contacted Melissa to do a story about her act of kindness and impact. Pictures from the event went viral on social media, catching the eyes of thousands, and her local TV station shared the story with tens of thousands of local people. When the dust settled, by purchasing 150 books to donate as graduation gifts for local seniors, Melissa left a lasting impression on 150 seniors and began building meaningful relationships with the students and their families. Over fifty thousand people in her community also saw her efforts in some capacity.

TODAY'S HOMEWORK

- ✔ Go back to your key relationships list.
- ✔ Highlight the school administrators, teachers, and board members on your list.
- ✔ On their school's website, look up the upcoming events for one that resonates with you.
- ✔ Choose one or two people and reach out to them.
  - ○ Let them know you're interested in donating to their school or volunteering to help with an event.
  - ○ Ask how you can help if you're open to the idea of getting out of your comfort zone with an open-ended question.
  - ○ If you know your availability and feel comfortable, ask about volunteering in the schools with specific days and times in mind.
- ✔ Take notes! You'll want to remember whom you talked to, when, and what you talked about. If you committed to helping during your conversation, put it in your calendar!

CHAPTER 8

THE INVOLVEMENT ADVANTAGE: SERVICE ORGANIZATIONS

THE INVOLVEMENT ADVANTAGE: SERVICE ORGANIZATIONS

Lisa was just a couple of years into owning her insurance and financial services agency. Like most new agents, she had begun by working through her "hot list" of friends and family—asking each to listen to her pitch and then (slightly awkwardly) asking for introductions to people they knew whom she might reach out to.

Lisa knew she had to expand her circle, but she wasn't sure how. One of her friends, Michelle, was the president of her community's Rotary Club. Michelle constantly asked Lisa to consider joining it, and as her connections began drying up, Lisa hesitantly agreed to attend their next lunch meeting.

Walking through the door for her first meeting, she noticed that there were only about twenty people in the room, and their average age was about sixty-three. Those who were still working were a couple of realtors, a funeral home director, a carpenter, the sales manager at a local car dealership, and even another financial service professional. The other members of the club were already retired.

The meeting discussion included a conversation on raising funds to help build a local dog park. Lisa did not have children of her own, but her dogs were her "fur babies." Lisa became excited about the dog park project and decided to donate some money to the cause. As the business portion of the meeting concluded, lunch was served, and Lisa was approached by the gentleman running the fundraiser for the park—a friendly retired man named Ed. They had a great conversation, and Ed invited Lisa to help participate in the actual building of the park once they got started.

A few months later, Ed reached out to Lisa and excitedly reminded her about the dog park project that would begin construction that Saturday. Lisa checked her schedule, and since she was available, she agreed to join the Rotary Club at the site.

Upon arrival, she saw many familiar faces from the meeting. All were happy that Lisa decided to join them. One of them was an elderly gentleman named John, who had to be close to ninety years old. He was dressed in old work clothes and a US Veteran ball cap. While John was there, he wasn't able to help much with the manual labor, but he did share plenty of laughs and endless stories. Everybody gravitated toward John and really liked him.

After spending the day with the local Rotarians, Lisa told Michelle that she would officially join the group. During the weeks and months that followed, Lisa showed up to as many of the lunch meetings as she could.

One day she got a call from the carpenter in the group. He was working on a house, and the homeowner mentioned needing to shop for a new insurance company. Immediately the carpenter thought of Lisa, and the connection was made. She was thankful but didn't think it was a big deal—just one introduction from her year in the club. *Not a great ROI on the outside*, she thought.

As she approached her second year as a member, the group hosted its annual officers' dinner. This was a formal event where spouses and different donors from the community could attend as well. Lisa and her husband sat at the same table as John, the elderly gentleman from the dog park. For the better part of two hours, they listened to John share his fascinating stories. Lisa kept asking him more and more questions, and he was happy to keep sharing.

The next morning, Lisa grabbed a greeting card and wrote John a note, thanking him for spending time with her and sharing his adventures.

A few months later, Lisa got a call from John. He asked if he could visit with her at the office.

"I always have time to meet with a friend, John."

THE INVOLVEMENT ADVANTAGE: SERVICE ORGANIZATIONS

John replied, "You mean an *old* friend."

Lisa laughed and reminded John that his spirit was still in its twenties!

When John arrived at Lisa's office, he was carrying a box of paperwork. As he began to unload it onto her desk, Lisa could see all his bank statements, insurance policies, and investment accounts.

"I need your help," he said. "I've worked my entire life to keep all of this straight, but now I need a professional."

John had three daughters, eight grandchildren, and over $10,000,000 in assets! He wanted Lisa to manage all of it and make certain everyone in his family would be properly protected and cared for after he was gone. A few weeks later, John became Lisa's biggest client. And it all started with a mediocre lunch she initially resisted and a $100 donation to a dog park.

KEEP AN OPEN MIND

Community service can set your small business apart from all the noise that happens when businesses fight for market share in traditional ways. While getting involved in community service can have many benefits, they really come when small business owners approach serving genuinely and with a sincere commitment to making a positive impact on the community. You know when someone is doing something for show and when it's an authentic effort. So do other folks.

You always want to lead with your heart.

You always want to lead with your heart. And while your efforts will likely create a positive impact on your business over time, it becomes *secondary* to the service you provide for your community.

Many times small business owners find themselves at a crossroads when deciding whether or not to get involved with local community service organizations and clubs. Just like Lisa, you may feel unsure about joining when you scope out the members at the first meeting you attend as a guest. Maybe you count twenty-five people and learn that five are from completely different industries and the other twenty are retired. And you start to feel like being a part of the organization isn't worth your time or that many are from your same industry and you feel late to the game.

There are long-term benefits of creating relationships with other members. I don't want you to become hyperfocused on how joining can exclusively grow your business. The focus of the Infinite Referral Advantage® is to expand your circle and create a connection economy. To do so, it's critical to think multiple steps beyond the immediate connection of a new relationship with a new customer.

Instead, consider ways your new relationship can benefit *someone else* in your network. Then you are able to make that connection. By doing so, the person you just connected with appreciates your efforts and is much more likely to reciprocate when the opportunity shows up.

The key here again is to choose clubs and organizations that align with your personal interests and passions. When you are involved first and foremost in furthering the mission of a group with the intent of making a positive impact, your willingness to keep pushing forward becomes much easier.

While your brain may initially gravitate toward local civic clubs and organizations when hearing the word *service*, it's imperative that you dig a little deeper. There are numerous industry-specific groups

THE INVOLVEMENT ADVANTAGE: SERVICE ORGANIZATIONS

to explore. These allow professionals within the same industry to join forces to support their community and network simultaneously.

Local Chambers of Commerce often organize community events and service projects. Small business owners can participate in these initiatives to give back to the community while building valuable connections with other local businesses.

You could also explore online platforms and communities dedicated to social impact or corporate social responsibility. Many businesses are now engaging in virtual service projects and connecting with like-minded individuals through online forums.

Many professional associations organize community service activities or have partnerships with charitable organizations. You can explore such opportunities within their respective industries.

Reach out to local nonprofits beyond the well-known service organizations. There are likely many smaller grassroots organizations with specific needs that align with the expertise and resources of businesses. I personally have strong ties with our local food bank, Catholic Charities, and the Feed Our Vets program. All these small groups provide tremendous—and much needed—support to my local community. Their mission aligns well with my personal values, and I'm proud to help as often as I can, both monetarily and with my time.

A SIMPLE YES CAN LEAD TO AN INCREDIBLE EXPERIENCE

Jump, and figure it out on the way down.

That's my approach when new opportunities arrive. Although it may seem impulsive or spontaneous, I've learned that some of my best experiences have come in the form of an unexpected invitation that I quickly accepted. I'm happy to share what I mean with a few examples below.

A friendly retired lady named Joanne visited my office one day asking if she could post a flier for an upcoming 5K charity run my town's school was hosting. We got talking, and after checking my calendar, I realized it was a Saturday morning and my wife, Kelly, and I were available to participate. I told Joanne that not only would I hang the flier, but I would be happy to donate items for their goodie bags and that my wife and I would sign up to run.

The day of the race was a blast! It was well organized and tons of fun.

Kelly and I stuck around afterward to help clean up. Joanne approached me explaining they had an open seat on their board. She wanted to know if I'd be interested in joining them.

"It's just one meeting a month and a few fundraising events like this one throughout the year," she promised with a smile.

With endorphins flooding my brain, clearly still feeling the effects of my runner's high, I answered without giving it much thought, "Sure!"

Just a few meetings into my new position on the school's foundation board, I met another board member named Gale. She was also on the Habitat for Humanity board. During one of our meetings, Gale shared a heart-wrenching story of a local family who experienced a devastating loss. It was just two weeks prior to Christmas when a hardworking family struggling to provide for three children and buy Christmas gifts lost their home to a massive fire.

Fortunately, nobody was home at the time, but they lost everything. For the past four months, they had been crammed into a hotel room. Habitat for Humanity was going to break ground on a new home for this family in a few weeks, and they were looking for volunteers.

THE INVOLVEMENT ADVANTAGE: SERVICE ORGANIZATIONS

My hand was already up before Gale finished the story.

The way Habitat projects work is that the family is required to be on-site to help build the home. Habitat hires professional contractors and then rallies a group of volunteers to defray some of the labor costs. My volunteer assignment on this project was hanging Sheetrock. If you've ever met me, you would know I'm not the handiest guy in the world. But I do have enough muscle to hold things in place, and with enough guidance, I can work basic tools such as an electric screwdriver. And that's what I did.

The best part of this assignment was the people I was working with. I had two of the children whose home we were building—Daniel and McKenna—with me the entire time. While putting up the walls to what would be their living room and bedrooms, I had the amazing opportunity to hear all about their future plans. We talked about where their beds would go, the types of posters they'd hang, and how to construct the perfect forts to hide from one another!

The family went through a horrific situation, but this new home they were helping to build themselves created new excitement and hope for their future. While it was only one week that I spent on the project, it was one that personally impacted me on the deepest level.

I told the children that when the house was complete, I wanted to be one of the first people to get a tour and I'd bring a special housewarming gift for each of them. As kids do, they remembered, and a week before the home was complete, they stopped by my office to give me a formal invitation to attend the ceremony when the front door was officially opened!

Please understand, from a business standpoint, I expected nothing in return for my efforts. I was proud to volunteer on this project. However, Gale introduced me to Pat, who was the local Habitat treasurer. After a brief conversation, Pat gave me the opportunity to insure not only this new home but all the homes in their portfolio. I did, and over the past ten years, I've not only had an impactful relationship with Habitat for Humanity, but I'm also the local chapter's insurance agent of choice.

Let's recap for a moment:

Joanne wanted to hang a flier for a 5K charity run. *I said yes.* I ended up on the school's foundation board, where I met Gale. Gale provided me the opportunity to get involved in heartwarming community projects where I met an amazing family. These projects connected me to Pat, who now introduces me to even more families each year. It's the Infinite Referral Advantage® at work. I wasn't thinking about getting involved. Instead, I just jumped in when the opportunity presented itself and started making meaningful connections. I ended up working on impactful community projects. And I had fun doing it too!

FIND YOUR FIT

My favorite pro tip for choosing the best service organizations to partner with is this: Do not overcommit. While it's easy to get involved, it's even easier to get overinvolved. I'm sure it won't shock you to learn that charitable organizations, nonprofits, and volunteer groups are always looking for your support.

Before making a choice, you need to get some clarity. Think about the answer to these questions:

- → What causes are you genuinely interested in or passionate about, and how much time and money are you willing to donate?

- If someone wanted to donate money to an organization on your behalf, where would you immediately want the money to go?
- If you took the day off to volunteer, what organization or cause would you give your time to?
- How much time do you regularly and realistically have to spend serving?

Once you have a clear understanding, you'll be able to share it during initial conversations regarding your level of commitment. Clarity is kindness—to everyone involved.

Use that information as you reach out to organizations and discuss getting involved. Clearly communicate your interest and availability. This helps the volunteer group plan schedules, activities, and projects effectively and keeps you from being overcommitted.

Consider volunteering for roles that align with your expertise. When you identify and leverage your skills, expertise, and interests as you serve, you can contribute meaningfully to the group while personally enjoying the volunteer experience. This also allows you to make a unique and valuable contribution to the organization and become known as the leader or expert in your field.

Participate in any orientation or training sessions provided. This equips you with the necessary knowledge and skills to contribute effectively while demonstrating your commitment.

Create positive relationships with fellow volunteers, staff, and leaders within the organization. Demonstrate reliability by fulfilling commitments and being punctual. Don't say you're going to do something without knowing with certainty that you can follow through.

Your reputation is on display anytime you are in the public eye. You represent your business, and your actions can either help or hurt your personal brand. Proactively seek feedback from the volunteer group, and be open to constructive criticism. Use it as a tool for continuous improvement in your role within the group and professional development as a small business owner.

Embrace flexibility and adaptability when faced with changes or unexpected challenges. Volunteers who can adjust to evolving circumstances contribute to the resilience of the volunteer group. This is also a valuable skill for your business too.

Don't keep quiet! Contribute ideas and collaborate with the group to improve processes or develop new initiatives.

EMPOWER YOUR TEAM

Large corporations have full human resource departments, offering larger base salaries, strong health benefits, retirement matches, flexible scheduling, or even work-from-home options. Chances are, as a small business owner, you are unable to compete with some or all of these perks.

One perk of working for a small business is the ability to give back to the community. Employees who want to do meaningful work will thrive in an environment that serves others well and makes a difference, regardless of the industry you're in. By creating this work environment, you'll find and keep more people like you—those who lead with a servant's heart—when you build community service opportunities into their role.

Ask employees about the causes and organizations they are passionate about. Then give them the time and space to do so! Provide them with the opportunity to shine in the community and build their personal brand while representing your business. This helps your employees feel more connected with your company and community and empowers them to lead and feel that their work matters. It also increases the pride they have for your business and improves the office culture.

You can decide if it's monthly, quarterly, biannually, or annually when you allow them to lead or get involved with a community project or service group. Provide them the opportunity to collaborate with others to give back. These can be individual efforts or, even better yet, team-building exercises.

Letting employees become involved with service projects on behalf of your business will improve engagement, job satisfaction, personal and professional development, retention, office culture, and recruiting efforts.

Remember, if you are not unique, you are weak. This applies when you are prospecting for new customers, but it also applies when you are seeking and keeping top talent!

MASTER THE ART OF COMPOUNDING RELATIONSHIPS

To build deeper relationships while serving, *always provide value first*. Proactively assist others in the group by sharing relevant resources, insights, or assistance tailored to their business needs. Present yourself authentically and generously, offering referrals without expecting reciprocation to demonstrate genuine support for others' success.

Seek out opportunities for collaboration on joint projects or initiatives. Working together on specific projects can lead to mutual referrals as well as a stronger professional bond. Share success stories related to collaborations or positive experiences with other businesses when possible. Positive testimonials and success stories can encourage others to refer to your business.

Stay informed about services and any changes in the businesses of your connections. This knowledge allows you to introduce clients or contacts to them when it aligns with their needs.

Use social media platforms to showcase your collaborations and support for other businesses. Host joint events or workshops with other small businesses. This not only enhances your visibility but also creates opportunities for cross-referrals. (There is more on this in chapter 10.)

Express gratitude for any referrals received. A simple thank-you note or a kind gesture can strengthen the relationship and encourage ongoing referrals. However, you don't want to stop at simple things. With this system, referrals are your biggest reward—so when you receive one, you want to make a *big* deal about it.

Share insights, and educate each other's networks about the unique aspects of your businesses. This knowledge empowers others to refer the right clients to you. You can offer a "lunch and learn" or other creative ways to share knowledge while expecting nothing in return.

Share regular newsletters or updates with your network. This keeps you on their radar, keeps you top of mind, and provides opportunities for them to refer you.

It's important to remember that it does not take a ton of relationships to expand your network. This is the practice of *compounding relationships*. It begins with a laserlike focus on a small group, and after building authentic, and genuine relationships with them, you are more likely to be introduced to their network.

Think of a snowball rolling down a hill. At the top, it fits in your hand. As it rolls down the hill, it picks up speed and grows just a tad larger with each rotation. By the time it reaches the bottom, it is taller than you are. The same principle applies here. What if one person led you to three more, then those three led to three more, and so on?

Let's look at the math:

1 × 3 = 3
3 × 3 = 9
9 × 3 = 27
27 × 3 = 81
81 × 3 = 243

Knowing that 1 relationship can lead you to 243 new introductions over time, the question becomes, "How many key relationships do you need to have?" The answer is, "Not many."

MEASURE THE RELATIONSHIPS YOU TREASURE

Don't forget that we seek the contrarian approach to traditional business systems whenever possible. With that in mind, when it comes to measuring results yielded from the Infinite Referral Advantage®, most will gravitate to the natural and obvious question: "How many referrals did I receive?" (Just like Lisa did at the beginning of this chapter.)

But I want to remind you, it's equally important to track your invisible results too. To go back to the gardening illustration for a minute, the big mistake small business owners make is planting the seeds one day and then basing their success on the harvest (or lack thereof) the next day. They lose sight of the fact that true success is found in the *cultivation* phase. It's certainly not one that should be skipped or hurried.

In fact, you can typically gauge a small business owner's level of success based on the timelines they think in. As a rule of thumb, those who need or expect results quickly are the ones who struggle. Whereas those who understand that long-term, sustainable results require long-term efforts (cultivation) are those who get to celebrate lasting success.

Obviously, the number of referrals received should be tracked. But the success of your efforts in this space cannot be determined quickly, and *leading indicators* should be measured first (a leading indicator is an action or activity that could potentially lead to the referral). Examples of these are as follows:

- The number of meaningful conversations had
- Number of "touches," or contacts, with people in the group
- Information gained that will be beneficial in the future
- How many introductions you sent to others
- If collaborative opportunities happened or if one in the works
- How many community events you participated in
- Number of social media posts and engagement
- Traditional media recognition
- Employee engagement and satisfaction
- Community awards or recognition
- Number of hours and money donated

If you are consistently doing and tracking all the leading activities over time (lengthening the cultivation process), the results will follow.

THE INVOLVEMENT ADVANTAGE: SERVICE ORGANIZATIONS

TODAY'S HOMEWORK

- ✔ Grab that key relationships list.
- ✔ Find the names of one or two people who are actively involved in service organizations that you'd be happy to be a part of.
- ✔ Look into two months ahead to see what their organizations have planned.
- ✔ Contact them, and let them know you're interested in helping at an event that interests you.
- ✔ Arrange to get your team involved.
- ✔ When the event ends, gather feedback—internally from the team and externally from those involved or warm markets who observed your participation.
- ✔ Based on what you enjoyed and learned, look at what's coming up the following month, and choose another service project.
- ✔ Again, take notes! Whom did you meet? What did you learn? Are there new people you'd like to add to your key relationships list? Go ahead and add them.

After a few months of jumping in on other projects, you'll have a good feel for the service groups and organizations you most enjoy working with and how your business is best suited to help. From there you can determine if you'd like to join forces with one in particular, collaborate with another group from the Infinite Referral Advantage˙, or create your own event.

CHAPTER 9

THE INTRODUCTION ADVANTAGE: STAR CUSTOMERS

THE INTRODUCTION ADVANTAGE: STAR CUSTOMERS

Early in my career, I suffered from imposter syndrome when it came to certain customers who, if I'm honest, felt a little intimidating to me. One of these customers was Kathryn. She was the CFO of a large healthcare company—intelligent, successful, and in charge. I was *extremely* nervous about her new customer onboarding appointment. I doubted my expertise and value, and I was afraid she would find the appointment boring and elementary.

She is in charge of the finances for a $100 million+ company, what could I possibly offer her regarding risk advisement?

She earned seven figures annually, traveled the world, and lived in a community with a gate. People like me weren't even allowed to drive on her street!

I assumed she already knew everything I knew, and I lost sight of the fact that regardless of how much she was worth or the title on her business card, people like Kathryn still put their pants on one leg at a time and faced the same struggles and challenges as everyone else in some capacity.

Not only did Kathryn find tremendous value in the insights I shared with her, but she truly seemed to enjoy the time spent at my agency.

At the end of the appointment (completely unprompted, mind you), she said to me, "Do you know who you remind me of? My friend Dave. I think the two of you would hit it off. I'm going to send you two an email to create a virtual introduction."

Here I had been considering canceling my appointment with Kathryn, and she ended up giving me a referral without asking.

Here is where the story gets even better:

Kathryn's friend Dave is the CEO of an international consulting company (successful people spend time with other successful people). Following the virtual introduction, Dave invited me to meet at his office. Kathryn was right—we did hit it off immediately. We had much in common, and our personalities meshed well. Our thirty minutes passed in the blink of an eye.

Before the meeting ended, Dave offered to let me have the floor in front of his employees at their next monthly meeting, and I happily agreed to bring lunch for his team of fifty. At this "lunch and learn," I spent twenty minutes educating Dave's team about managing risk, industry insights, and the benefits of doing business with my agency.

While standing in front of Dave's employees, I discovered that he had a gift for hiring amazing people just like him. I shared my calendar and let his employees choose a ten-minute block of time to have a deeper conversation about their personal insurance needs. Of the fifty people in attendance, thirty-four of them requested a call.

To recap:

One thirty-minute meeting with Kathryn led to a thirty-minute meeting with Dave, which led to thirty-four scheduled calls with prospective new customers. *Total cost?* About an hour and a half of my time and a few hundred dollars for a buffet-style lunch.

Beyond the numbers and amplified ROI, the customers acquired from Dave's business are some of the best customers I have today. And guess what? They've also led me to even more people just like them. *Connectors* love to connect people to others!

HAPPY CUSTOMERS EQUAL HAPPY REFERRALS

Many small business owners do not have a plan to leverage one of the most impactful marketing sources there is: *happy customers!* As a general rule, people surround themselves with people who are like

THE INTRODUCTION ADVANTAGE: STAR CUSTOMERS

themselves. So the types of customers you desire are typically friends with others who are also the type of customers you desire.

Jim Rohn once said, "You're the average of the five people you spend the most time with."

If this is true, then once you meet an amazing customer, it's likely there are four others in their network that you'd enjoy meeting too.

You can spend countless dollars on cold, generic marketing ads, but in this modern-day world, you are who your Google reviews say you are. People trust the feedback from friends, family, and neighbors far more than advertising agencies.

> **Authentic customer testimonials build credibility and trust among potential customers.**

Authentic customer testimonials build credibility and trust among potential customers. And they are more likely to believe the words of someone who has no vested interest in promoting a business. Speaking of *no vested interest*, happy customers are willing to be unpaid sales people for you!

Knowing this, it is important for small businesses to create a space for people to share these testimonials and positive experiences. It's also imperative that the business shares the importance of such feedback with its customers. Ultimately, people want to help those who serve them at a high level. Oftentimes they don't *because they don't know how to.*

When customers are highly satisfied, they are more likely to be in a positive emotional state. This positivity increases the chances of them introducing you to people they know. Look for moments when customers just experienced exceptional service or received a high-quality product they are excited about. Being present with customers in some capacity during these moments ensures that the positive experience is fresh in their minds. While this system is designed to have customers and key community relationships send you referrals without asking, it is important that they understand that referrals are important to you.

When you boil down a referral conversation, there are two ways to go about it. You can ask people directly for names and phone numbers of people they know. *Yuck.* Or you can mention that referrals are important to you through casual conversation (without the cringe). This is another chance to plant some seeds.

When you are present when a customer is extremely happy with you, your company, your products, or your services, you may simply thank them by sharing some version of this:

"Sarah, I can't thank you enough for doing business with us. We know you have numerous options out there for (insert your product or service here), so we are grateful for your trust and support. In fact, we are trying to build this business around awesome people just like you! So if you come across anyone else we can help, it would be so awesome if you shared your experience with them."

Sarah had a positive experience, she's a customer who trusts you, and it's fresh in her mind, so plant the seed. In that sample above, I never put Sarah on the spot, made her feel uncomfortable, or directly asked her to give me names and phone numbers (that's all cringy). Instead, I expressed gratitude, acknowledged that she had other choices, complimented her for being an awesome person, and then encouraged her to share her experience if she felt so inclined.

Customers are most likely to refer at these moments:

- After the initial sale
- Following positive feedback, they are sharing without solicitation
- After you resolve an issue

THE INTRODUCTION ADVANTAGE: STAR CUSTOMERS

- When they achieve a milestone
- After they leave a review or testimonial
- During annual reviews or client appreciation events
- When completing a satisfaction survey

Other ways to plant seeds are by saying things like the following:

- "Don't keep us a secret."
- "Spread the word!"
- "We are people helping people."
- "The greatest compliment we receive from our customers are introductions to people they know."

When first meeting a potential customer, ask, "Who referred you to our business?" You'll get one of two answers: (A) the name of the person who referred them—awesome! or (B) they'll give you a funny look and explain that nobody did.

This provides you the opportunity to share that you work almost exclusively off referrals from happy customers. The reason you were asking is because you give customers who refer others a small gift as a token of appreciation. This plants the referral seed before you even dive into the sales process.

But, Scott, I have great customers who just aren't into referrals. What do I do then?

Some people simply are not comfortable referring people they know to others. Regardless of how much value you offer, many people fear that making a referral or recommendation will backfire on them if the interaction doesn't go well.

There are people who place high value on the privacy of their friends and family. While certain star customers may love you personally, they don't feel comfortable bridging that conversation with those in their network. When you encounter people like this, it's important that you respect their decision to not introduce you to others.

This does not change the level of service you provide and the value you offer. Just because these customers will not proactively recommend you, it doesn't mean that they won't when directly asked for a recommendation from a friend.

Sometimes there is just a lack of communication or awareness with customers. While it's our goal to receive referrals without asking, that does not mean we are passive. It is possible to make it clear that you value introductions from others without specifically asking for one.

PUT YOUR SMALL BUSINESS SPIN ON CORPORATE STRATEGIES

Some corporate Goliaths have done an incredible job creating high customer loyalty and brand ambassadors. I'll bet you know them quite well.

Apple has a loyal customer base that often feels a sense of exclusivity and identity with the brand. Their design, innovation, and overall experience have created a community of Apple enthusiasts who will often wait hours in line to purchase their latest product. Apple users argue that their product is far superior to the competition's and passionately defend it when others disagree. As an Apple customer myself, I feel inclined to share with you that this book is being typed using a MacBook, the best laptop on the market today.

Starbucks built a global community brand around its coffee culture. The Starbucks experience, along with personalized rewards

THE INTRODUCTION ADVANTAGE: STAR CUSTOMERS

and a sense of community, often has its customers waiting in line ten times longer to order from their barista versus stopping at a competitor who has no wait time.

Harley-Davidson motorcycles have a strong following, creating a sense of camaraderie among motorcycle enthusiasts. The brand represents a lifestyle, and customers often feel a deep connection to the community. When a Harley rider passes another Harley rider on the street, they wave to one another to acknowledge this connection. When they pass the rider of a motorcycle that isn't a Harley, there is no wave—because they aren't one of them.

Disney has a multigenerational fan base that feels a deep connection to the magic and nostalgia associated with the brand. By creating such a magical experience, people will make a Disney vacation a bucket list item. Loyal members are proud to be part of the Disney vacation club, so they guarantee themselves a Disney vacation annually and have the opportunity to pass that along to future generations.

So the question becomes, "How?"

How did Apple, Starbucks, Harley-Davidson, and Disney create such brand loyalty and turn their customers into brand ambassadors? How did they create a customer base so fiercely loyal that they passionately promote the brand?

And how can you do the same in your small business?

Here you go:

1. **Don't be a "one-trick pony."** It all starts with quality products and services. Let's be real—you can have the most amazing marketing plan, top salespeople, and an A+ customer experience, but if the product or service you are selling is a dud, you won't last long. The out-of-business graveyard is filled with examples. So make certain your products and services are top-notch first.

The more products and features a customer has from you, the happier and more loyal they are. Think of a six-foot-long two-by-four piece of wood that you need affixed to a wall. When you hammer a nail into the center of it (your core product), it will be stuck to the wall, but it won't be tightly secured. When you add an additional product, service, or feature (a nail to the left side of the board), it becomes more secure. Another product, service, or feature (a nail to the right side of the board), and it becomes more secure yet. The more nails into that board, the stronger the two-by-four's bond is to the wall.

With Apple, I use their iPhone, iPad, MacBook, AirPods, watch, music, and Apple Pay. I have their app, a user ID, and a login to the website. Needless to say, I'm affixed rather tightly to their wall.

How many products, services, and features can you offer your customers to complement your core offer? And finally, remember my mantra: "If you're not unique, you're weak." What does your business do differently than everyone else? If you don't have a list of at least three things that separate your customer experience from the competition, you won't stand out. And if you don't stand out, you become a commodity (something a customer can buy from anyone, anywhere, and it makes no difference who). Just like Apple, "Be different." How you do that is up to you.

2. **Take inventory of your customer experience.** Enter your facility with the lens of a customer. What do you see, smell, and hear? How do the lighting and the temperature make you feel? How are your customers greeted? Oftentimes it's difficult to see areas of improvement when you're personally committed and close to something. It may be helpful to ask a friend for assistance. Have them visit your business as a customer (or prospective customer) and share their feedback with you. Ask them to be brutally honest, and stay open to their feedback.

What can you do that will make each customer experience unique and cause them to feel special? Personally, I try to accomplish this with a variety of drinks and snacks. Each guest we have gets to pick out their favorite to enjoy while they are with us. We also have company swag to hand out; this way nobody leaves empty-handed. This could be something as simple as a pen, notepad, chip clip, or can koozie. Each year customers receive handwritten birthday cards from our team, and we actively seek other life events (marriage, birth of a child, illness, or passing of a loved one) to send a handwritten card.

The easiest and most cost-effective way to make an impact on a customer is by addressing them by name throughout your conversation and expressing gratitude. The very first gift we received on earth was our name. To customize a conversation, be sure to speak their name often. This demonstrates that you recognize and acknowledge them as an individual, making the interaction more meaningful and personalized.

Gratitude is also a zero-cost, high-return tool at your disposal. Something as genuine and simple as, "Jennifer, we recognize you have numerous options out there when it comes to (insert your product or service here), I just want you to know we appreciate you choosing us. Thank you!" can go a long way. Expressing your gratitude can be the conclusion of a face-to-face interaction, a voice mail, an email, or a text. Never pass up on the opportunity to leave a customer with the "warm and fuzzies."

If you can offer a customer loyalty program, *do it!* If you can offer a gift in exchange for a customer introduction, *do it!* The key to a referral rewards program is not to lead with it. This means that when a customer does introduce you to someone they know, thank them and *then* share the details of your program. I always keep gifts within my network. If one of my key relationships is a pizzeria owner who is a loyal customer and consistently introduces me to their network, then I will purchase gift cards from their pizzeria to give as gifts to my customers who refer others to me. One of my other mantras is, "We are people helping people." You support my small business by introducing me to somebody you know, and in return, I support someone else's small business so you can enjoy their products or services. It's a virtuous pay-it-forward circle.

3. **Create a customer culture that supports your brand.** Are your customers proud and excited to do business with you because they feel like they're part of something special? My agency's mission statement begins with "It's our mission to be different. We accomplish this by doing things that others don't and others won't." I believe in being direct and creating clarity. If you want people to know something specific about you, don't hint at it—*just say it*. Then, you have to back it up.

   So for my business to be different, I have to consistently deliver on my promise of uniqueness. I want my customers to trust us, respect us, but also see us as friends—people they can have fun with and feel special because *they're our customers*. When you keep your focus on these core principles, you build a tribe of customers who are proud to do business with you. It's a level of loyalty where they get defensive when others say they have a good insurance agent. They'll respond with, "Maybe, but I have the *best* one!"

   Are customers able to engage with you outside your business? This piggybacks off of community events from the last chapter. You can also hold customer appreciation events to give you the opportunity to have fun and interact with your customers (like a ball game, summer picnic, or winter carnival).

   What can you do to create generational customers? During my new customer onboarding process, I gather information for the children in the family. I make it my mission to recognize their birthdays and meaningful events in their lives such as academic, athletic, musical, or any other achievements. As much as people appreciate receiving thoughtful cards in the mail for themselves, those feelings get amplified when you acknowledge their children. The more you can incorporate entire families into the customer experience, the better!

This is a long-term play. But there is nothing better than a new customer who is proud to do business with you because their parents always did and as a child they remembered being a part of that experience too.

4. **Develop a compelling brand story that communicates the values, journey, and mission of your business.** Don't shy away from sharing the challenges and struggles you face in addition to the success and passion behind your brand. This will create a narrative that will resonate with customers. Remember that telling is not selling.

People make buying decisions based on emotion, not logic. Therefore, the more compelling your stories are, the more customers will gravitate to you. Feature customer success stories and testimonials. These real-life experiences of how your products and services positively impact customers will create relatable and emotional connections.

Produce authentic and genuine content that reflects the personality of your brand and your team members. And finally, pull back the curtain and share behind-the-scenes moments of your business. Whether it's showcasing your workspace, introducing team members, or revealing insights into what makes you different, these glimpses will humanize your brand and strengthen emotional connections.

THE INTRODUCTION ADVANTAGE: STAR CUSTOMERS

To ensure consistent quality, you must establish clear and measurable standards for products, services, systems, processes, and customer experience. Each quarter perform quality control checks to identify any deviations from the standards you have set.

Those four companies I mentioned have achieved remarkable customer loyalty. They transformed customers into brand ambassadors by delivering outstanding products, services, and experiences while fostering emotional connections and creating a sense of community.

Strategic marketing campaigns, consistent branding, and a focus on customer engagement have played crucial roles in building and sustaining brand loyalty. As a small business owner, you are able to implement these proven practices to generate your own Infinite Referral Advantage˙.

CREATE AND CULTIVATE STAR CUSTOMERS

Immediately following a customer purchasing your products or services is the best time to demonstrate to them that they made a fantastic decision by choosing you. Clearly, they like and trust your business; otherwise, they would not have made a purchase. Knowing this, you want to validate their decision by spending more time with them. The onboarding or welcome appointment allows you to get to know your new customer on a deeper level and better understand their needs.

During that meeting, you can set the expectations for future communications. Find out how they prefer to be contacted (call, text, email, or other). Explain how often you'd like to meet with them going forward (annually or every other year) so you can keep up with their busy lives and ever-changing needs. This way you can offer helpful suggestions and solutions in the future as well. Encourage them to connect with you and your business on social media or subscribe to your newsletter. If you have online services or an app, make sure they are digitally connected to you as well.

Remember, the more value you add to people's lives, the more likely they are to introduce you to others. Top-of-mind awareness is created by having customers see and hear from you consistently. Because you cannot personally be in all places, having conversations with customers all the time, it's crucial that you leverage technology. Emails, newsletters, and social posts will keep you relevant.

Engage star customers in collaborative goal-setting sessions. Align their personal objectives with yours, and explore how the partnership can contribute to mutual success. Shared goals create a sense of shared ownership and purpose.

Assign dedicated account managers or customer success representatives to star customers. Having a personalized point of contact ensures that their needs are understood and addressed, fostering a stronger connection.

Actively seek feedback on how the partnership can be improved. Demonstrate a commitment to continuous improvement based on their input. This collaborative approach reinforces the idea that their feedback is not only valued but actively used to enhance the partnership.

Identify the star customers who have a strong track record of successful engagements, loyalty, and a good understanding of your products or services. These customers are likely to provide valuable insights.

THE INTRODUCTION ADVANTAGE: STAR CUSTOMERS

Clearly communicate the purpose and vision of the introduction-focused initiatives (why referrals are important). Share your business mission and goals as well as how these initiatives align with the mutual success of both your business and the customers.

In your CRM, have a space dedicated to the Infinite Referral Advantage® category your star customer falls into:

- → Do they own or work for a small business?
- → Do they work in or are involved with schools at some level?
- → Are they involved with nonprofit, volunteer, community service, or civic organizations? Are they active on social media?
- → Are they somebody who has a large audience and is seen as a thought leader or influencer?

Once you have each star customer categorized, you can diversify your efforts accordingly.

TODAY'S HOMEWORK

- ✔ Review your current client lists to identify any new names you can add to your list of key relationships.

- ✔ Create a customer satisfaction survey. Use it during the new customer onboarding welcome meeting and each time you meet with current customers (annually or every other year). Keep the survey short (five to seven questions). You can find samples of each at www.referralsdonerightbook.com/bonus.

- ✔ In the final questions, you should ask about overall satisfaction and the likelihood of them introducing others to your business. Based on these responses, you know how referable your business is through the eyes of your customers.

- ✔ Track the number of referrals generated from your star customers, along with their conversion rate. You will find that while the volume of new prospects you receive from customer referrals may be lower than traditional marketing, these new opportunities will convert into customers at a much higher level.

- ✔ Perhaps most important is tracking the customer lifetime value (CLV) from customer referrals. A higher CLV for referral customers indicates the long-term value and profitability of this strategy.

CHAPTER TEN

THE INFLUENCE ADVANTAGE: SOCIAL ENGAGEMENT

Some people see social media as the land of make-believe, where people can pretend to be anything they want. Others see it as the place only to share a highlight reel—the best five minutes out of the 1,440 in each day. I've also seen the *incredibly positive* impact social media can have on people, small businesses, and communities.

When you live in the state of New York, at times you deal with heavy snow or freezing-cold temperatures. Hurricanes, however, are not typically a concern. That changed in October of 2012. Hurricane Sandy was an extremely large and destructive category 3 Atlantic hurricane that ravaged the Caribbean and the coastal Mid-Atlantic region of the United States. It was the largest Atlantic hurricane on record as measured by diameter, with tropical storm–force winds spanning 1,150 miles.

The evening of October 29, Monday, Sandy slammed into New York and New Jersey head-on with winds of eighty miles per hour. Sixty-nine thousand residential units were damaged, thousands of New Yorkers were temporarily displaced, forty-four perished, and the financial impact was north of $19 billion.

Five days later, I sat at my kitchen island, morning coffee in one hand, scrolling Facebook on my phone with the other. I read through a post from a friend of mine whose sister's community was severely impacted. The story shocked me. They had no power, no heat, and no running water.

Grocery stores were closed, making it impossible to purchase food. Displaced neighbors were finding shelter wherever they could. The scene was that of a third world country, but my friend was describing a neighborhood in New York City—just a few hours south of where I sat. The post went on to share a list of essential items people needed in his sister's neighborhood.

THE INFLUENCE ADVANTAGE: SOCIAL ENGAGEMENT

It was one of those moments when I felt inclined to jump in and help. Without giving it a second thought, I shared my friend's post. In my post, I offered my insurance agency as a drop-off location for anyone who wanted to donate. My agency had been open for just over two years. At that time I was renting a nine-hundred-square-foot office space with four employees in it. My friend was heading down to Long Island on Friday with donations from our area. So we had four days to collect some essential items: flashlights, lamps, batteries, warm clothing, jackets, hats, gloves, bottled water, non-perishable food, and cleaning supplies.

In my mind, we would collect some items Monday through Thursday, and then on Friday, I could drive them over to my friend, who was renting a U-Haul to deliver them to his sister's community.

I quickly learned that I not only underestimated the heart and support of my community, I underestimated my ability to influence it.

When I arrived at my agency at eight o'clock on Monday morning, there was a line of people waiting at the front door (I assumed correctly—they weren't all there to purchase insurance policies) with boxes filled with donations. Two hours later, our small reception area and kitchen were completely filled with donations. The phone was ringing off the hook from people asking how they could help. Vehicle after vehicle kept pulling into our parking lot as my heart raced and my brain scrambled for a solution to the massive outpouring of generosity that was overtaking the office space all at once.

Well, Facebook clearly helped spread the word initially, so I went back to it and shared the situation (complete with pictures of my small office busting at the seams). Within minutes another friend who leased a large warehouse called me and offered his space—*sold*!

With the storage problem solved, I moved on to the next problem—transportation. I found myself back on Facebook, asking for help from anyone who owned a truck. Within minutes I had a crew of trucks en route to transport boxes from my office to the warehouse space about five miles down the road.

I canceled all my appointments for the day and went into full-blown logistical manager mode. Some people dropped off items without boxes, so I requested some empty boxes. Several elderly people had donations at their homes that needed to be picked up, so I made house calls.

As boxes piled up at the warehouse, we realized there was no order to them, so I assembled a team of people to unpack and categorize the donations (so we could repack later). Around seven o'clock PM that evening, I realized I never stopped to eat lunch and clearly didn't make it home for dinner. I muscled my way through one more hour, and after twelve hours of work, I dragged myself home to crash.

As wild as Monday was, Tuesday was even busier. Word was spreading that my team and I were leading the charge on local donations. The volume of donations *doubled* on day 2! I continuously recruited and managed teams of volunteers. We had a receiving team, a transportation team, a sorting team, a purchasing team (we were receiving thousands of dollars daily in donations), a team of people coordinating volunteers, and oh yeah, then there was my agency team doing their best to serve our customers throughout it all. Monday's shift of 8:00 a.m. to 8:00 p.m. was stretched to 7:00 a.m. to 9:00 p.m. on Tuesday.

Then, on Wednesday morning, calls started coming in from the local schools. All had been taking collections from students and their families. *We needed more trucks!* Six local schools each required pickup trucks to fill with donations. Wednesday's shift was from 6:30 a.m. to 10:00 p.m. day. Thursday was the same, but with a Friday delivery day looming, the final packaging had to happen that evening. It was just after midnight when the final box was taped shut and labeled. It was the end of an eighteen-hour day, which capped off four consecutive days of work, and I had to be back six hours later.

It was four days and over fifty hours of intense mental and physical labor. That evening (or early morning as it were), my head hit the pillow, and I began to cry. I wasn't sad. I had never cried for "no reason" before. I was confused, but I couldn't stop sobbing. Clearly, I was emotionally overwhelmed, malnourished, dehydrated, and absolutely *exhausted.*

My friend who was heading down to deliver everything was blown away by our efforts and the generosity of the community. He received a donation from a local Freightliner company, a fifty-three-foot-long tractor-trailer. It arrived at our warehouse at six o'clock Friday morning, and our crew of volunteers created a human chain, passing boxes down the line and filling the truck. *And fill it we did!* All fifty-three feet—front to back, top to bottom. There wasn't room for an additional box of tissues—which was good because we needed them.

My friend asked if I wanted to take a ride down with him to meet the people who would receive everything we worked so hard to collect. I didn't have it in me. After breaking down emotionally a few hours earlier, I simply knew I couldn't handle making that trip. The tractor-trailer pulled away, and I took a deep breath and smiled. I drove back to my agency, walked in, looked at the team, and laughed. "Well, we managed to collect a few things, huh?"

Sometimes you just jump and figure it out on the way down.

When I offered to help, the last thing I was thinking about was my business, personal branding, or the Infinite Referral Advantage®. However, when all the dust had settled that week, I had connected and worked side by side with dozens of fellow small business owners, all the local schools, community service groups, and hundreds of my customers. And I leveraged social media to communicate details while highlighting the efforts of so many amazing people along the way.

My personal investment was losing a week of production at the agency, forfeiting sleep, and some gas money. My return on investment was established leadership, relevance, respectability, and a vastly expanded network of those who mattered most in my community.

WORK-LIFE BALANCE IS A MYTH

Prior to owning my own business, I strived to create a work-life balance. When I was at work, I focused all my energy there—even at the expense of my own family and things that brought me happiness. And when I was not at work, I focused all my energy there—no work thoughts were to be had until that Sunday night when anxiety kicked in.

For many years after opening my first business, I struggled to find that balance—and for good reason. For the small business owner, it doesn't exist!

Hear me when I say this: *It's okay that it doesn't!*

Let's break this down:

You started down the path you're on now because you have a true passion for the products and services you offer. In fact, knowing that you're still reading this proves to me that you want to help more people in more ways. So if your passion and purpose align with your core values, and you truly believe that everyone needs to learn about your offerings, and every day you are excited to be the person who gets to share this message with others—*is that really work?*

During an interview with fellow SBO Lisa Briggs (Fit Body Bootcamp, Whitesboro, New York), she shared, "I believe the old cliché 'When you love what you do, you never work a day in your life' is wrong." Lisa went on to explain, "When you love what you do, you spend your days *working harder.*"

Those words resonated with me.

I realized that early in my career, I was telling myself I was out of balance if there weren't specific blocks of time forcing me to completely detach from work. Now, don't misunderstand, I'm not advising anyone to ignore family, friends, wellness, and self-care at the expense of work. In fact, I do not subscribe to the "grind and hustle" culture either. The thought process of "Nobody cares, work harder" looks great on a coffee mug, but it can lead to overwhelm and burnout as well.

The question I'm posing here is, "Why do work and play need to be separate?" The entire premise of giving your business the Infinite Referral Advantage® is centered around creating and strengthening relationships. What better way to develop and strengthen relationships than having fun with people outside of work?

Let's connect the dots:

You love the work you do; that's why you are passionate about doing it every day. You love your family, your friends, your customers, and the community you serve. You are going to be out and about doing things you enjoy when you aren't physically at your business anyhow. You want people to see you as the sincere, genuine, authentic person that you are. And you aren't going to see everyone every time you go out. So why not share your experiences on social media so others can experience them with you?

The biggest mistake I made with social media was becoming too one-dimensional. Not wanting to share my business life with my personal network and my personal life with my business network stunted the growth of my brand. I was trying to be two different people, and doing so made me less authentic. If your personal values align with your business values, there's only one way to live your life.

YES, DEAR INTROVERTS, YOU CAN BE ON SOCIAL MEDIA

I understand that being on social media doesn't feel natural for everyone. In fact, it wasn't for me at first either! I reluctantly created my first social media account in 2009. The entire experience was awkward and unnatural. However, so was starting my own business.

Ultimately, I knew that if I was going to meet the number of people I needed to work with to provide the volume of products and services I needed, I couldn't keep my personal brand and business a secret. In fact, there aren't many businesses that can survive without people knowing about them. So embrace it. You don't have to love it, you should absolutely put your own flavor to it, but what you cannot do is ignore it.

I'll be the first to admit that I consider myself an introvert. If I get invited to a big networking event, I'll begin by shuffling through the door and taking it all in before I find a couple of people I'm comfortable with. Then I can enjoy myself. At networking events,

I'm not a life-of-the-party kind of guy, *and that's okay with me.* I refuse to be anyone other than who I am. And I expect nothing less of you than to be yourself at all times.

But here is the beauty of social media. When I'm at the event, I can take some pictures of the catering, the venue, the people who invited me, and what they were celebrating or the cause they were raising funds for. Then I can create posts talking about each of them, lifting them up, and tagging them so I can share the impact they had on me with my audience and theirs. Maybe I talked to three or four people out of the hundred or so who were there, but then I took the opportunity to talk to thousands more in a heartfelt way with a few taps of my phone.

My wife, Kelly, and I host the *Love Living Local 315* Podcast. Every Monday we pick five or six local businesses that we visited during the previous week, and we just talk to each other about it. We share our experiences and what our family liked about the places we went to for about fifteen minutes. Then we tag all the small business owners.

Wednesdays are reserved for our "Hey, Neighbor" segment, where we invite local guests who are doing awesome things. And on Thursdays, we do what we call the "Weekend Buzz," to highlight upcoming events in our community.

It isn't overwhelming or draining for us to sit down and tell people about the things we're enjoying about our community by having our own conversations. We get to share our thoughts with thousands of people through our microphones. By doing so, we add value to our key relationships by shining the spotlight on them and the awesome work they are doing. It blurs the lines once again between work and life, and that's how we like it.

CREATE AUTHENTIC RELATIONSHIPS ONLINE

The tipping point for my consulting business occurred in the spring of 2020 (probably not surprising to anyone who lived through that year). In the fall of 2019, I was so tired. Tired of living out of hotels, dining at airport bars, speaking in stuffy conference rooms without windows, cramming work in at 35,000 feet, and saying good night to my wife and children over the phone rather than hugging them in person.

In November of 2019, I locked myself into a studio and recorded all the content that I had been traveling the country to share. The following sixty days were spent crafting months and months of weekly lessons that could be delivered live utilizing Zoom. Insurance Agency Optimization kicked off 2020 as a completely virtual training platform, with new content being delivered daily and a weekly cadence of live video calls. As you read this now, you may be thinking, *So what, Scott? Everybody does that.* And you'd be right, but almost nobody in my space was doing this pre-Covid.

By the end of March, businesses had nearly all their employees working from home, planes were grounded, schools were closed, and people were spending more time in their homes than they had ever dreamed. Insurance was an essential industry. So while agencies had their doors locked, they still had to produce new policies while servicing their current customers. Owners of insurance agencies were scrambling to navigate this new world without physically seeing their employees on a daily basis. And here I was with a robust virtual training platform that pushed into everyone's homes so they could continuously learn and improve while trapped on lockdown.

Business exploded!

THE INFLUENCE ADVANTAGE: SOCIAL ENGAGEMENT

I share this because for the two years that followed, I met, worked closely with, and developed deep relationships with over one thousand people *whom I had never actually met in person*. It was a complete one-eighty from how we operated in the past. In fact, to this day, I have never been in the same physical space as many of my peers and clients whom I consider great friends. In between our Zoom calls, emails, texts, and phone conversations, I follow them all on social media.

One such friend immediately comes to mind. His name is Chris.

Have you ever met somebody for the first time and just felt like you know them? Well, how crazy would it be to have never met a person, but not only feel like you know them but feel as if you know *everything* about them? That's how I feel about Chris.

He's a family man who owns multiple community-based small businesses. He works over fifty hours each week—not because he has to, but because he wants to. Chris is a proud University of Washington alumni and a big fan of the San Francisco 49ers. He travels to Europe with his wife twice a year, and he had an extensive corporate career in management prior to opening his first business.

He enjoys fast food more than he should. He's outrageously proud of the community he serves and has a deep passion for sharing lessons from prior experiences that will help fellow entrepreneurs. He struggles with stress, anxiety, and some ghosts from the past, which now motivates him as he pushes forward.

I know all about Chris. I like Chris. I learn from Chris. I root for Chris.

I have never met Chris in person.

That's the power of social media.

Here is how Chris was able to connect with thousands of people just like me who thoroughly enjoy following him on social media, and what we can learn from him:

1. **Be authentic, genuine, and transparent in your interactions.** Share behind-the-scenes content and personal stories to humanize you and your brand. There is a fine line between living in the land of make-believe and creating a reputation as a negative Nancy. It's absolutely okay to share your highlight reel with others, but it's just as important to share your struggles.

2. **Maintain a consistent tone and personality across all your social media platforms.** Who are you? Who do you want to be known as? It's an odd exercise, but also a wildly effective one: write your own obituary. In five hundred words or less, pen to the masses how you want to be remembered and the things you were most proud of accomplishing after the dust settles on your life. This is a form of vision-boarding, you are creating an avatar for the person you want to be. Now share that person with the world while you're still here. You'll remain consistent by continuously asking yourself, "Is this a post, message, or picture that Future Me would be proud of?"

3. **Ensure that your personal brand voice aligns with your values and resonates with your target audience.** Actively engage with your audience. Respond promptly to comments, messages, and mentions. Ask questions, seek feedback, and encourage discussions to create a two-way conversation. Encourage your followers to create and share content related to your brand.

4. **Showcase User-Generated Content (UGC) to highlight your community and strengthen the sense of belonging.** Share informative, entertaining, and valuable content that addresses your audience's interests and needs. Foster a sense of belonging and shared identity among your followers. In the insurance world, the business owner might post a picture of their "why" when it comes to life insurance and protecting their assets. This might be a picture of their children as an example. Then they ask the audience to share their "why." A real estate agent might post a picture of their favorite room in the house and share all the things they love about that room, then encourage people to post their favorite room or the type of room they'd love to have in their next home. A life coach might ask the question, "What is something you were fearful of as a child that you no longer are? Or still are?" These types of posts encourage UGC, create engagement, and allow you to get to know/understand their audience on a deeper level—as the audience gets to know them as well.

5. **Tailor your content to the preferences and interests of your audience.** My best advice would be to meet people where they are. Know which demographics are most active on which platforms. The younger generation prefers short-form content found on TikTok and Instagram; X will allow the opportunity for quick thoughts and insights; the middle-aged to older crowd is on Facebook; and, for your "over fifty" target who enjoys longer form, perhaps it's a written blog via a consistent email campaign and also shared through a Facebook group. Use data to segment your audience and deliver personalized experiences. Occasionally, surprise your followers with exclusive content, giveaways, or special events. Show appreciation for your followers through shoutouts or recognition.

6. **Connect emotionally with your audience through storytelling.** Share compelling narratives about your brand, products, team, or relevant stories from your personal life. While your products and services might make sense logically, people make buying decisions based on emotion.

7. **Stay consistent!** Remember, our goal is to be contrarian. In order to do so, we have to understand what the masses are doing so we can be different. Most small businesses are sporadic with their posts. So to be different, you need to establish a social media calendar. This way your audience gets used to a specific cadence from you and begins to anticipate or look forward to your content. Also, from an algorithm standpoint, the more your audience engages with your posts, the more you will continuously show up as they scroll.

8. **Customize and personalize content as often as possible.** In a crowded digital space, you have to cut through the clutter. Posts that blend in with the masses get passed by. Highlight the people, places, and things that do not normally get attention. Everyone is posting about the latest trend, the movie stars, and athletes that are currently dominating the headlines. You now understand the Infinite Referral Advantage® and how shining a spotlight on fellow small business owners, schools, service groups, and your star customers creates a win-win situation. So dive deeper into those stories and post unique content specifically designed about people in your community that your neighbors will appreciate.

9. **Be aware of the dates and times that you post.** If you have an amazing thought at 1:00 a.m. on a Tuesday, don't jump out of bed and reach for your phone (although you may want to write it down). Save that thought for a more optimal time to post. When is that? It truly depends on your audience. Keep track of engagement and how different posts perform at different times of the day. Create consistency around campaigns though. For instance, if you are going to post a daily thought, remain consistent with time. If it's 9:00 a.m. one day, 10:30 a.m. the next, and 8:00 a.m. the next, this confuses the audience. Most people have morning routines, so changing your post times for recurring campaigns will lose them.

I can't stress it enough. To be relevant in this modern business world, you must remain consistently active on social media. As humans, we are able to see the same thing and have differing views on what we are looking at.

So is social media a blessing or a curse? It certainly could be either. But when done right (and that's the only way you should want to do anything), it's one of the most tremendous marketing and branding tools available to an SBO today!

No longer are we at the mercy of traditional media to determine if our products, services, efforts in the community and success stories are "newsworthy." Today we are the media. You get to decide what is newsworthy in your world and regarding your business. You get to create the narrative, provide the content, and share your own personal insights. You get to create, and demonstrate the strong, personal, reputable, influential brand that your audience gets to know, love, and engage with. And it costs close to nothing to make it all happen. What a blessing!

But if you still aren't convinced that you can keep up with a consistent schedule, I'll encourage you to tap into an excellent source of relationship marketers—high school or college students looking for an internship! They have the skill, ability, and time to connect your businesses to other businesses, students, service groups, and potential customers at community events and over social media.

TODAY'S HOMEWORK

- ✔ Evaluate your social media options. (If you aren't already.)
  - ○ Explore online platforms, such as LinkedIn, where professionals meet and connect. Begin to focus your attention on the one where your ideal customers spend time.
  - ○ Search for individuals or businesses in your target industry and reach out to establish key relationships.
- ✔ Review your numbers. Is your social media audience growing? That's the goal, and it's also the easiest metric to track. No different than how we track profits, losses, revenue, and expenses, SBOs should be tracking net gains or losses with their social media audience. And there's no better time to start than now.
  - ○ Dive into the engagement metrics. Track the number of likes, shares, and comments on your posts.
  - ○ Or find someone who loves this kind of stuff, and outsource this task to them!

THE INFLUENCE ADVANTAGE: SOCIAL ENGAGEMENT

- ✔ Attend networking events. Go to industry-specific events, conferences, and meetups.
  - ○ Engage in conversations, build relationships, and exchange contact information with potential key relationships. If your social media handles aren't on every marketing material you have, make plans to change that soon.
  - ○ "Piggybacking" with other people's events is great. However, fellow SBO Marvin Manns often shares, "You can go to an event, or you can *be* the event." If you feel inclined, you can certainly create and host a big, splashy event of your own. Whatever you decide, just be sure to post online about it. Most events have less than one hundred in attendance. Once shared on social, now thousands get to see you there!

CHAPTER 11

MAINTAINING YOUR INFINITE REFERRAL ADVANTAGE®

∞

Early on in owning my business, I was chaperoning my son's first-grade field trip when a fellow parent—whom I'd never met—approached me and said, "I know you, you're the insurance guy!"

Well, I was, but I didn't know who *he* was.

He went on to say, "You must be doing all right for yourself."

As a small business owner, you know how loaded those words can feel, especially when you're first starting out. Any form of "You must be doing well," "It must be nice," or (my least favorite) "You're so lucky" makes a new small business owner want to vomit.

So there I was, waiting for the reason why this gentleman who met me for the first time believed I must be doing all right for myself.

"I see you all over the place!"

MAINTAINING YOUR INFINITE REFERRAL ADVANTAGE®

Internally, I was anything but doing well for myself—I was a mess. However, it was at that moment that I knew I was a mess who was *on the right track*.

That gentleman completed his thought with this:

"I ordered a pizza, and your flier was on the box. I walked into the coffee shop, and your picture was on the board. When I ate at the local diner, they brought the bill, and the pen I signed with had your information on it. Then I saw you passing out trophies to the kids at the football game last weekend. I got on social media and who did I see? *You.* I was getting my haircut, and my barber told me you're the guy to see for insurance. Now I'm at the zoo with my daughter, and I finally get to meet you in person! I guess I should probably give you a call soon to see if you can help with my insurance."

At that moment, everything changed for me.

Everything that gentleman mentioned wasn't a result of massive marketing expenditures or an overbooked schedule (I mean, I was chaperoning a school field trip), but they resulted from the relationships I had created with small business owners, schools, community service groups, my star customers, and social media.

I was elated. My plan was working!

Now, not only was that an incredibly validating experience, it was fun too. A person I had never met *already knew me*. I didn't have to mention what I do or ask him if he would consider doing business with me. He already wanted to do business with me, and all I did was listen to him. I guess I was "doing all right for myself" after all.

SLOW AND STEADY HAS A HIGH ROI

Developing authentic, value-based business relationships doesn't happen in an instant. It takes time. Building trust, understanding, and mutual benefits takes persistence and continuous effort throughout the entire life cycle of the relationship. The good news is that hundreds of years of history have proven that *nearly all* your competitors will not take the time or put in the effort to build these meaningful relationships. This is why your willingness to do so gives you such an incredible advantage.

William Butler Yeats, winner of the Nobel Prize for literature in 1923, said, "A stranger is a friend you haven't met yet."[1] It was true over a hundred years ago and remains true today. Every friend you have, each relationship you hold dear, and the people you trust today are all people that you did not know at some point in the past.

I find it interesting that so many small business owners neglect this vital piece of the marketing puzzle, stating they don't know how or have the time. Every small business owner *does* know how and is already spending time doing things that involve other people. What the Infinite Referral Advantage® provides is structure, intentionality, and consistency.

This process requires patience and persistence. There truly is no shortcut to success, and that is especially true when it comes to building trust and creating loyalty. Every small business owner would gladly take two steps backward today if it meant taking five steps forward in the future.

The transition into this process may initially feel as if you are taking those two steps back. So it's important to keep your eye on the prize, which is *lifetime value*. Customer lifetime value (CLV) and key relationship lifetime value (KRLV) both go beyond a single transaction or moment in time. Relationship building requires time and effort, but the return on investment is significant.

Strong and loyal customer and referral bases contribute to sustainable revenue streams and business stability that can last a lifetime. So those two steps you take "backward" by using this process won't actually equal five steps forward, but rather *five hundred* or more over time. The key is to get the process started—which requires some discomfort, focus, and effort. Then, once you have it established, you get to engage autopilot—when the process becomes fun, fulfilling, and extremely lucrative.

The flywheel effect is a concept popularized by Jim Collins in his book *Good to Great*. It represents the idea that organizations, like a massive flywheel, require substantial initial effort to get moving. Once in motion, the flywheel builds momentum, making it easier to sustain and even accelerate over time.[2]

The key is consistency and persistent effort.

In this context, the flywheel effect is associated with meaningful contacts with key relationships, creating a cumulative advantage, and the compounding benefits of consistent actions. Here are just a few examples of daily occurrences that can happen when you adopt the Infinite Referral Advantage® and make it your own:

- A fellow small business owner shared content with their audience on social media calling you an expert in your field.
- You get invited to speak or share at events of key relationships.
- A key relationship asks you to sit on boards or committees.
- You are nominated for or receive awards or certificates for your efforts.
- People in your network call you for advice or to seek introductions to others.

- People leave you unsolicited online reviews or provide testimonials.
- People are proud to be a part of your network and gladly wear your merchandise or display your swag.
- People recognize you without having to be introduced.
- You receive personalized gifts from KRs.
- The traditional media contacts you for interviews for market or community insights.
- Employees have a greater sense of pride working at your business
- Customer retention or repeat sale rates increase. (You also receive feedback that customers choose or stick with you even though others offer similar products and services for less money.)
- Your KR list grows month after month.
- You begin to have to turn down community or collaboration opportunities because there are too many.
- Your online reviews and social audience grow month after month.

STEP 1: START WITH A MANAGEABLE KR LIST

You've been working on your key relationships list, chapter by chapter. Now it's time to narrow it down to your initial twenty people. Your list will grow to more than twenty over time, but for the vast majority of you, starting with twenty is the best way to initiate the method.

Take out that list of your initial list of KRs. Review it and see if you have at least one person in each of the five categories. It's perfectly fine if you have more small business owners and fewer school administrators, or vice versa. You have to start with a level of comfortability, or instead of collecting referrals, this list will just be collecting dust.

When my list began, I initially started by focusing on key relationships with people who were on my level (young, inexperienced, struggling). Then my list expanded to include more successful people and professionals. Today my key relationships include corporate executives, chairs of boards, presidents of large organizations, locally and nationally known politicians, authors, writers, speakers, thought leaders, and cutting-edge innovators.

Each year that I remained consistent with this process, my key relationships leveled up. As a result, I leveled up as a professional. Without even realizing it, I went from admiring best-selling authors, TEDx Talk speakers, and seven-figure entrepreneurs to being one myself.

Be sure to list people you respect and can learn from. Seek people who have already accomplished the things you want to achieve. Always be evaluating and elevating your list. Successful people are connectors by nature. They are always eager to say things like, "Do you know whom you have to meet?" And then they introduce you to that person.

STEP 2: CREATE YOUR KR CALENDAR

Now that you know the twenty people you're ready to serve and create (or intentionally continue) a relationship with, it's time to get yourself organized. The best way to keep track of your connections is by working with your new best friend, the KR calendar.

Ready? Oh yes, you are!

The KR calendar is a useful tool for you to plan your intentional connections with the folks in your Infinite Referral Advantage®. Once you establish your list and integrate it with the KR calendar, you'll know exactly what to do, when to do it, and for whom you're doing it. Keep your calendar as simple as possible.

To build your calendar, first, take your simplified KR list of twenty. Label each one with a letter of the alphabet starting with *A: Name #1, B: Name #2*, and so on. So with twenty connections, your list will run from *A* to *T*.

MONDAY	TUESDAY	WEDNESDAY	THURSDAY	FRIDAY
A 1	B 2	C 3	D 4	E 5
F 8	G 9	H 10	I 11	J 12
K 15	L 16	M 17	N 18	O 19
P 22	Q 23	R 24	S 25	T 26
A 29	B 30			

MAINTAINING YOUR INFINITE REFERRAL ADVANTAGE®

Write your first key relationship on the first line in the *A* box, next on the first line in the B box, and so on. If you have more than twenty key relationships (that's awesome!), don't add letters to the list, just go back to the top, add a second name to the *A* box, and keep doubling up as far as needed.

Next, decide which day you are going to start bringing your Infinite Referral Advantage® to life (pro tip: *pick TODAY*). The day you begin, you will label *A;* the following day is *B*; and you keep going until you reach the letter *T* (day 20); and then the following day is *A* again. The goal is to create meaningful contact with each of your key relationships once every four weeks. Keep in mind, this assumes a Monday-to-Friday cycle and does not include holidays.

Don't lose sight of the compounding nature of this system. You'll start with twenty KRs, and your list will grow from there. Also, if you have team members creating their own advantages as well, their list of twenty will grow too.

With you and three team members all consistently spending twenty minutes each day focused on one key relationship each, that's eighty meaningful contacts every four weeks. After a year, your efforts will have compounded into 1,040 contacts—and it only requires twenty minutes each day from a total of four people. That is what leveraging time and relationships becomes with consistent focus and effort. *Insert a mic drop right here.*

STEP 3: CHOOSE YOUR TOUCHPOINTS

Information is the new currency in the business world, especially when it comes to building and strengthening relationships. The more you know about a person, the deeper your sense of connection, trust, and understanding forms. Knowing about a person's interests, preferences, and life events allows you to tailor your interactions to align with the things that matter to them the most. You can create effective communication by personalizing conversations, written communication, and unique gift-giving once you are equipped with information. I like to call these interactions touchpoints. Here are some of my favorites:

- In-person visits to get to know them
- Handwritten cards
- Leaving 5-star reviews
- Emails letting them know what you value about the business that caused you to write them a 5-star Google review

Other touchpoint ideas include connecting with them on social media, making introductions, and creating opportunities for collaboration. You can view our entire touchpoints checklist at www.referralsdonerightbook.com/bonus.

With traditional marketing, getting in front of others is very expensive. A billboard in Times Square costs much more than one on a rural road. Space at the top of Google search results costs money, as opposed to being buried on page 3 for free. The goal of the Infinite Referral Advantage® is to create top-of-mind awareness, trust, and opportunities without breaking the bank. By digging deeper with key relationships, you receive quality prospects over a high quantity of cold leads.

It's natural to look at bottom-line results while evaluating time and money spent on marketing. However, relationship marketing is different. Traditional marketing offers the opportunity to spend money, create an advertisement, blast it on a specific platform, and then calculate results.

In a new relationship, this would be the equivalent of going on a first dinner date and proposing before the entrée is served. It would be weird, unnatural, and premature. Shockingly, you might actually get a handful out of a hundred to say yes to that approach (assuming your ask is extremely compelling), but then would you want that type of spontaneous person as a lifelong partner?

There's a natural order to everything in life. When it comes to your top twenty key relationships, the most important piece of the evaluation puzzle is information.

- How much have they shared with you?
- Do they respond to your written communication?
- Do they engage with your content on social media?
- Do your in-person conversations feel comfortable and natural?
- What are they passionate about?
- Do your interests and values align?

Don't trust your memory. Make notes after every interaction, and document everything!

STEP 4: STAY ON TOP OF YOUR TOUCHPOINTS WITH TIME BLOCKING

We all get 1,440 minutes each day. Is it realistic for you to dedicate twenty of those minutes to focus on important aspects of your business? *Of course it is!* That's just over one percent of your day. Time blocking is a strategy that continues to help me and my team stay on top of my key relationships. Here are some of my favorite tips on time blocking:

- **Choose a consistent time.** Select a time slot that is consistent and feasible for you every day. This could be in the morning before work, during lunch, or in the evening. Consistency is key to forming a habit.

- **Use a calendar or planner.** Utilize a calendar or planner to mark and block the twenty-minute time slot each day. This visual representation helps reinforce the commitment and serves as a reminder.

- **Communicate boundaries.** Inform colleagues, family members, or anyone who might be affected about your designated time. Setting clear boundaries helps avoid interruptions during your dedicated twenty minutes.

- **Eliminate distractions.** Create a focused environment by minimizing distractions during the allotted time. Turn off notifications, close unnecessary tabs or apps, and inform others that you're not to be disturbed.

- **Start small, and build gradually.** If dedicating twenty minutes seems challenging initially, start with a smaller time frame and gradually increase it. Building a habit takes time, and starting small increases the likelihood of success.

MAINTAINING YOUR INFINITE REFERRAL ADVANTAGE®

- **Reward yourself.** Establish a reward system for completing your twenty-minute sessions consistently. This could be a small treat, a break, or any form of positive reinforcement to motivate yourself. I use a momentum calendar to visually chart consecutive day streaks.
- **Reflect and adjust.** Regularly reflect on your progress, and adjust if needed. If the chosen time slot proves inconvenient or if the activity needs modification, be flexible in adapting your plan.
- **Be realistic.** Set realistic expectations for what you can achieve in twenty minutes. Avoid overwhelming yourself with an unrealistic workload, and ensure that the goal is attainable within the allotted time.
- **Accountability partner.** Consider having an accountability partner who can check in on your progress and provide support. Sharing your goals with someone else increases the likelihood of commitment.
- **Track your success.** Keep a record of your daily accomplishments during the twenty-minute sessions. Tracking your success reinforces the habit and provides a sense of achievement.
- **Evaluate and adjust over time.** Regularly evaluate your commitment to the daily twenty-minute activity. If needed, adjust the time slot, the nature of the activity, or any other elements to better suit your schedule and preferences.

Use your time blocks to update the key relationship rubric (below); plan and schedule the upcoming touchpoints for the day; and if time allows, take immediate action (if it's something quick such as sending a handwritten card).

Track your winning streaks as you complete your daily time-blocked activities. Give yourself a little immediate reward for taking action and getting things done.

Track metrics such as the following:

- → The number of contacts you made
- → The amount of information you gathered for the KR rubric
- → Positive feedback, compliments, and KRs mentioning, tagging, or engaging with you on social media
- → Thoughts, ideas, suggestions, or collaboration ideas from a KR
- → Introductions made to others
- → Potential customers referred

STEP 5: REVIEW YOUR KRS

Okay, Scott, how do I keep up with my KRs when all the letters on my calendar are overflowing with people for me to maintain authentic relationships with?

But there's nothing like a group of people who truly enjoy each other's company and want to help each other.

I'm so glad you asked! Let me introduce the key relationship rubric. This is a way for you to collect pertinent information and make informed decisions based on that information. Think of it this way: you are the president of your own "cool kids club." These are the people you enjoy networking with and sharing your life with. That means, there is probably someone on your KR calendar that isn't a good fit for you, that's okay. These are real relationships, and you may not be everyone's cup of tea. Me either. But there's nothing like a group of people who truly enjoy each other's company and want to help each other.

Don't lose sight of the number-one goal of all marketing: top-of-mind awareness. Relationship marketing is no different. You want to get the right eyeballs on you and your brand, at the right moments, so that when they need your products and services, you are one of the first small business owners they think of.

Essential components of your KR rubric are the following:

- **Clarification:** Clearly understand the purpose and objectives of each key relationship. Define what you aim to achieve and how the partnership aligns with your overall business goals. Are you looking for direct referrals primarily? Do you hope this person will connect you to others in their network? Would you like this person to mentor/guide you professionally? Will this relationship improve your brand and increase your credibility? Can this relationship lead to collaborative efforts or cross-promotions? Do you want to be introduced to this KR's social audience?

- **Segmentation:** Categorize your relationships (fellow SBO, school, service, customer, social acquaintance). Evaluate factors such as importance, strategic alignment, and potential impact on your goals.

- **Prioritization:** Not all KRs will be equally important, and some will be more important during different phases and seasons of your business. Prioritize relationships based on their significance to your business objectives. Allocate time and resources accordingly.

Here is an example of a KR rubric that you can adapt to your needs.

KEY RELATIONSHIP RUBRIC

Touchpoint Results

Date of communication:
Communication approach (in-person visit, in-person collaboration, in-person shared event, handwritten card, text, email, social media engagement, gift, value-add presentation, online review, etc.):
Detailed notes from communication:
Date for next contact (refer to your KR calendar for this):
Plan for next type of communication:

KR Professional Profile

Name:
What is the KR's role?
Professional background?
How long have they been where they are now?
What is KR's knowledge and expertise in their industry?
What market insights can they provide?
What are the KR's professional goals?
Company goals?
How does the KR prefer to communicate?
What level of decision-making authority does the KR have within their organization?

What are their personal interests or hobbies outside of work?

Do they participate in networking events?

Is the KR involved with civic or charitable organizations?

Are they actively involved in community or social causes?

What challenges or pain points does the KR face professionally?

How can you potentially help?

Are certain times of the day or month preferred when meeting?

Review their professional profiles on platforms like LinkedIn; they can offer insights into their career trajectory and professional interests:

Identify public endorsements, projects, or achievements shared on social media. Provide topics for positive conversations:

Understanding their involvement in professional associations or industry networks. Provide additional points of connection:

Know their preferences regarding networking events or conferences. Could this help in suggesting relevant opportunities?

KR Personal Profile

→ **Family structure**: If this person is married, has children, or lives with family can provide insight into their lifestyle and potential priorities.

- **Educational background**: Knowledge of their educational background helps in understanding their expertise and areas of specialization.

- **Personal interests**: Learning about their interests and hobbies outside of work can provide opportunities for casual conversations and shared activities.

- **Leisure Activities**: Understanding how they spend their leisure time helps in finding common ground beyond the business context.

- **Travel habits**: How often do they travel? What types of trips do they enjoy?

- **Frequent destinations**: Knowing if they have regular travel destinations can provide conversation topics and potential meeting opportunities

- **Wellness practices**: Awareness of any wellness practices or routines they follow can guide conversations about well-being.

- **Health considerations**: If relevant and appropriate, understanding any health considerations can inform how you can accommodate their well-being in the collaboration.

- **Gift preferences**: If considering gifts or gestures, knowing their preferences or restrictions ensures that your gestures are thoughtful and will be well received.

- **Cultural sensitivity**: Be aware of cultural considerations when selecting gifts or planning gestures to avoid unintentional misunderstandings.

Evaluation (Rate on a scale of 1-5 or mark N/A.)

→ **Communication effectiveness**: Assess how frequently you communicate with the KR and the quality of those interactions. Regular, open, and clear communication is indicative of a strong relationship.

→ **Level of collaboration:** Measure the degree of collaboration on projects, initiatives, or shared goals. A strong relationship often involves active participation and joint efforts.

→ **Consistency**: Assess the consistency of the KR in reciprocating communication. A strong relationship is built on trust, and consistent follow-through is a key indicator.

→ **Trustworthiness in confidential matters:** Consider how trustworthy the other party is in handling confidential information. Trust is foundational to a strong business relationship.

→ **Alignment of values**: Assess the alignment of values with the KR. Shared values contribute to a more cohesive and enduring business relationship.

→ **Common goals**: Identify whether you and the KR share common short-term and long-term goals. A shared vision enhances the strength of the relationship.

→ **Duration of relationship:** How long have you communicated with this KR? A long-standing partnership often indicates mutual trust and satisfaction.

Results:

Referrals this KR has made to my business:
Introductions KR has made to other potential KRs:

COMMIT TO THE LONG GAME

Here is the funny thing about time . . . it just keeps going. With or without us, whether we feel ready or not, time doesn't care—it doesn't discriminate. In one-second intervals, it never quits marching ahead. So the question becomes, *will you march with it?* Or will you allow it to march on without you?

Life is a game. The fun part is, you get to decide how the score is kept. You will keep track of the personal metrics that are important to you. However, the clock is out of your control. Everyone playing the game of life has the same clock on their scoreboard.

Unlike a traditional clock—yours counts up, not down. It started doing so the moment you were born. One second at a time, sixty seconds in a minute, sixty minutes in an hour, twenty-four hours in a day, and it never stops ticking up, second by second. As you already know, the tricky part is that everyone's clock will stop once it hits a certain number of days. The thrill is that everyone playing this game has no idea when their stoppage time is. So the true goal of the game is to work quickly and efficiently to rack up your desired score before time expires. There truly isn't a second to waste because you cannot get them back, and there's no stopping the clock—it just keeps going. With or without you. Ready or not.

The business world is no different.

It's a game within the game of life, and it uses the same clock. In business, you get to control the metrics that get tracked. So if life is a game, business is a game, and time cannot be stopped, everyone involved lands in one of three categories either by choice or default:

- **Spectators:** These are individuals who watch an event, activity, or performance without actively participating in it. Spectators watch the participants from a distance and judge the performance of those who are actively involved. Some spectators want to participate; others do not; but regardless of internal desires, spectators simply watch others.

- **Casual players:** These are individuals who play the game occasionally—mostly for fun, and without a serious competitive commitment. Casual players have varying degrees of interest in the game. Some participate recreationally; others have a deeper level of interest; and for some, it's a passion. However, all casual players draw the line at making the game the thing they become known for. While they take pleasure in occasional participation and even experience high-level success at times, they stop short of making a full-time commitment.

- **Professional players:** These are individuals who compete with consistency at the highest level—it's their livelihood. Professional players dedicate a substantial amount of time, effort, and commitment to honing their skills to achieve success in their chosen field. This group is committed to their craft and prioritizes their chosen activity as a primary focus in their lives. Professionals exhibit discipline in their routines and choices. They love to compete and win, so they are always looking for an advantage to help them accomplish this.

I already know which category you are in.

Spectators never would have started this book. Casual players would have read up to the point where they realized there'd be some work involved. The professionals—*you*—are still here at the end.

Why?

Because you take your craft seriously. You believe that if you are going to the game, you might as well play. And if you are going to play, you might as well win.

As a business professional wanting to win and looking for an advantage, you know there is one of three ways to attack a new concept—or level up with a concept you already recognize as valuable.

1. **Do it yourself.** This book allows you to take the Infinite Referral Advantage® and run with it. I've given you all the tools. Now you can apply them with consistency and grow your small business through authentic service and relationships.

2. **Do it with a little help from a friend.** Find a small business owner whose drive matches yours and become accountability partners. Set goals and meet weekly to check in and celebrate your small victories together. Then keep going!

3. **Outsource it.** You may not be the right person for this job. That's okay. Delegate to, or hire, someone who is. As they implement this system, they will earn their salary and more for your business!

NEED HELP KEEPING UP? WE HAVE A SYSTEM FOR THAT!

If you like what you've learned but would like some extra help, a personal consultant, or access to other exclusive benefits, I can help!

As this system worked for me, I was not only thrilled to teach it but also developed proprietary software that offers a plug-and-play approach to helping you deploy your Infinite Referral Advantage®. This CRM software is an automated system that small business owners can subscribe to, manage, and analyze their interactions with each key relationship. With a primary goal of enhancing relationships and streamlining processes, it can help you improve your consistency as you make, track, and ultimately follow up with connections.

Once you build your top twenty KR list, it gets uploaded into the software, which can help you keep track of the following:

- **YOUR KEY RELATIONSHIP CONTACT INFORMATION**

    Contact details, all previous interactions, referral history, personal preferences, notes, and reminders for upcoming opportunities

- **LEAD MANAGEMENT**

    Tracking and managing potential new key relationships in the pipeline, from initial contact forward

- **REPORTING AND ANALYTICS**

    Generating reports and analytics on key relationship behavior, referrals, collaborations, and other key metrics to inform strategic decision-making

→ **CONSISTENT CONTACT AUTOMATION**

Follow-up reminders and suggestions for new touchpoints to streamline your key relationships calendar on the four-week cycle process

→ **COMMUNITY EVENTS**

Managing and tracking upcoming event opportunities

→ **SOCIAL MEDIA CALENDARS**

Giving you consistency with industry-based and personal suggestions for growing your audience and expanding your reach

The software won't contact school administrators, post on social media, or send a card for you. But it will save you time, guide you along this proven framework, and streamline the system for whoever is building your Infinite Referral Advantage® for you.

Now you've got all the tools needed to build your own Infinite Referral Advantage®, you know how to use them, and they are all packaged into an easy-to-use toolbox we call the KR list and KR calendar. Now it's time to get to work and help build the business you dreamed of through authentic, value-driven, engaged relationships with the people, organizations, and places you care about. Chapter 12 will give you two more tools essential to elevate your advantage even more.

WWW.REFERRALSDONERIGHT.APP

CHAPTER 12

GRIT AND FAITH

∞

Nick spent the early years of his web design career jumping from job to job. He enjoyed the work he was doing, but not the corporate constraints. Nick knew having a boss wasn't for him, and the only way he'd find meaning and purpose in his work would be to start his own business, so he took the leap of faith.

The benefits of being a small business owner were great in regards to the freedom to make decisions and set the direction for his company. Nick didn't miss having to answer to higher corporate authorities either. This autonomy allowed for more flexibility in implementing creative ideas and strategies.

However, Nick's income dropped drastically, especially during his first year. His ability to land new clients was sporadic at best. Nick was in the early stages of building key relationships with fellow small business owners who could potentially use his services when he started to grow frustrated.

I've been working with Nick for the past seven years, helping him navigate the Infinite Referral Advantage® with the grit and faith required to realize the long-term results he desires. In my professional bio, I refer to myself as a coach and consultant, but honestly, I'm more of an informal counselor. I help clients work through the mental warfare that comes with owning a small business and maintaining relationships with people.

Nick knew and understood the system within weeks. He spent months putting in the work to get in front of key relationships. For years he has remained consistent with meaningful contacts and creating top-of-mind awareness. While there have certainly been many wins along the way, just recently he had a breakthrough.

Perhaps it was pure coincidence, or maybe it was the universe validating our work together in conjunction with the ending of this book. As I penned this final chapter to encourage you to maintain grit and keep the faith with this process, I received this text from Nick:

> I literally have new clients flying in. I'm struggling to keep up, there are so many, but it's given me a new jolt of energy for the business. I also just had one of my key relationships leave his job to start his own web business—he just sent me an email asking if I'd consider collaborating with him on some big projects he's landed. Then, one of my best customers just shared a huge plug for me on all of his social media channels. It's wild how all of this is happening at once. I'm struggling to keep up with the email requests that are coming in. What a great problem to have!

GRIT AND FAITH

I was so excited for Nick! I immediately asked if I could share his success to close out this book. For the past seven years, Nick put in the work. We would communicate several times each week sharing thoughts, ideas, wins and misses, but mostly encouragement. Encouragement to keep working through this process with daily consistency even though tangible results weren't visible.

As I read Nick's message over and over and over again, the words that jumped out at me were, *"It's wild how all of this is happening at once."*

I've seen this time and time again from those who commit to the Infinite Referral Advantage® system. Those who stick with the grit and keep the faith ultimately find that tipping point and experience a breakthrough.

I first experienced this in my own business. Today I make minor adjustments by pulling certain levers to fine-tune my Infinite Referral Advantage®, but mostly, I just stay out of the way so it can do its thing! When I read Nick's message, I smiled because I knew his "snowball" had now reached a size and gained a speed where he'd no longer be able to keep up with it.

Wild? Perhaps to Nick. It wasn't wild to me though.

An advantage? No doubt.

The result of sticking with a strategic and intentional process? Absolutely!

But it's a story that never gets told without grit and faith throughout the process.

ELIMINATE THE SIN IN YOUR LIFE

You understand that to win with consistency against bigger opponents, you need to compete differently. Anytime you don't conform to the masses, people will question and judge you. Anytime you don't get immediate results, you will question *yourself*. And once you begin to question yourself, the thoughts and opinions of others who doubted you begin to feel like validation that they were right.

Suddenly, voices of SIN inside your head increase in volume, in the form of **S**elf-doubt, **I**nner criticism, and **N**egative self-talk. You may notice thinking things like, "I'm not a strong relationship builder," "I'm not worthy of being introduced to other people's networks," "My products and services are not that valuable," "The people I want to connect with already have people they refer to," or "I've tried to establish this Infinite Referral Advantage®, and it just does not work for me."

That voice in your head gets louder and louder, and those self-defeating statements grow stronger and stronger, to the point you start to believe they're true—so you listen to them. This is when most people will quit. My challenge to you is this: replace ***quit*** with ***grit***.

Because I prefer to take complex situations and simplify them, here is my definition of *grit*: *keep doing all the things you know you need to do, even when you don't see desired results and you want to quit.*

Writer Robin Sharma explains, "What you focus on grows, what you think about expands, and what you dwell upon determines your destiny."[1]

If you're consistent with your SIN, you'll start to see more examples to back up what you're thinking. But if you continue to remind yourself that you're playing the long game, planting seeds, and rolling that little snowball down the hill to gain momentum and reap the benefits later, it will serve as a helpful reminder that you are, in fact, on the right track.

A disproportionate ratio of obstacles and temptations will present themselves daily. It's easy to find reasons to skip the work. All around you are people and programs offering shortcuts to success. Nobody will blame you for conforming to the norm. There is nothing the masses of average people love more than good company!

Putting in the work is difficult. Fighting through obstacles and naysayers with the grit required to accomplish your goals is hard. But so too is not meeting the standards you've set for yourself. Settling for a life of mediocrity and a professional career that gets overshadowed by those willing to do the work will leave you in a funk.

So you have to choose your hard.

Which challenging path will you choose to navigate each day? The one that delays present gratification for long-term fulfillment? Or the one that delays present-day work for long-term frustration?

My simplistic approach to *faith* is *"a person's ability to see invisible results."* When you are doing all the things that you know will eventually get you to the places you want to be, but you aren't realizing results, that's hard.

Your grit propels you to travel down that hard path, and faith will keep you focused to stay on it. With the Infinite Referral Advantage®, you are one introduction away from turning faith into fact.

Once a key relationship connects you to others, your questions will turn to confidence. This will fuel you to remain consistent with the process until you reach a tipping point where your results double your efforts. But until then, grit and faith will guide you.

Business is a game. Finding the success you desire in business is mental warfare—with battles being fought daily. Those who learn to control their minds will control their results.

Those who play the game at the highest levels understand there are only two basic rules: **start and finish**.

Go ahead and read that last sentence again. You probably thought you read it wrong the first time. *Start and finish? Really? Is that the groundbreaking, earth-shattering insight I stuck around until the final chapter to receive?*

Actually, yes. Yes, it is. I'll expand.

People will often wait years to start an activity that only takes minutes to complete. Starting a new task, system, process, or habit is daunting and can be downright scary. It requires change, and just behind death, public speaking, heights, spiders, and snakes, you'll find *change* on the list of things that scare humans the most.

People will stay in situations they know are bad because they fear change even worse. So what's the result? Many never start. Thousands of people will spend hours reading this book cover to cover, they'll leave 5-star reviews (thank you), they'll share it with their friends (much appreciated), but then they won't start building their own Infinite Referral Advantage® by listing their key relationships.

They fear change, so they won't start.

The good news is that thousands *will* start!

However, when obstacles pop up (and they will), when naysayers laugh (and they will), and that voice in their head gets louder and louder (and it will), most will quit. They will quit on their grit and bail on faith.

Why?

Because quitting is easier.

So they extend the hard path by jumping back to the starting line of something new, which seems easier. The highway of disappointment is jammed with perpetual starters. Those who hit roadblocks, rather than figuring out how to move past them, go back to the beginning with a new road map. Spoiler alert, that map will eventually lead to obstacles as well.

Have the courage to *start*, the *grit* to work your plan daily, and the *faith* to keep going even when everyone and everything around you says you should quit.

A diverse group of fellow small business owners, schools, service groups, star customers, and the social media outlets to highlight them all.

These deep, meaningful relationships arm you to do battle with corporate behemoths. Your sincere desire to serve your community by pouring value into others gives you the *advantage* to win with consistency.

Your willingness to operate with grit and faith, refusing to quit, allows you to play this game for as long as you choose—forever if you'd like. You never have to ask anyone for anything, yet people want to give you everything.

That's how referrals are done right.

That's what it means to have the Infinite Referral Advantage®!

OWN YOUR ADVANTAGE

You are no longer the underdog in this fight. You now have the upper hand. In your pouch are five stones, and each of them is useful, but together they are lethal.

You have the Infinite Referral Advantage®. And now you have the strength and courage to launch it.

In the words of Malcolm Gladwell, "The true story lesson for all of us to learn from the story of David and Goliath is that giants are not as strong as they seem. And sometimes the shepherd boy has a sling in his pocket."[2]

You have five stones, a plan, and a willingness to work your craft and improve your accuracy consistently. You have to—your livelihood depends on it.

You have deep, meaningful relationships with key individuals in five diverse areas. You know and care about the customers you serve and the prospects you seek. While your competition unloads

GRIT AND FAITH

their ammunition with tremendous force, at a high volume, all of it sails over the heads of those in your network—it's white noise.

They know it's there, but since they don't acknowledge it, they stop seeing and hearing it over time. They don't need the products and services your competition offers because they already have you. You are the one with the upper hand—the relationships that were built on value and trust. You have the *advantage*. The giants are the true underdogs.

Small businesses have been the backbone of our economy since the beginning of time. Because we aren't seen on a national level, and we aren't ten times the size, there is a perceived weakness. However, those who play the game to their advantage win with consistency. Which would you rather have—ten one-dimensional, well-known giants or a thousand crafty, persistent, skilled shepherds? There's power in numbers, and when we all team up, we become an unstoppable force.

- When small businesses team up to serve one another, they all grow stronger.
- When small businesses pour value into schools, the next generation grows stronger.
- When small businesses partner with local service groups, communities grow stronger.
- When small businesses recognize the needs of customers by acknowledging their support with gratitude, brand loyalty grows stronger.
- And when we share all this positivity with others by leveraging social platforms, our servant's hearts are validated, and the mission grows stronger.

This system does not require a month-to-month restart. This is not a limited-time marketing campaign. This is our DNA. It's who we are as small business owners. By leveraging meaningful relationships, we are a force to be reckoned with. Our success is not a once-in-a-while event; it's a daily commitment—one that has no end. Once our focus on relationships is initiated, our results have no limits—they are infinite.

The day David offered to fight Goliath wasn't his first time using his sling. He had committed years of work to become deadly accurate so he could safeguard his family's livelihood and their flock. If birds, bears, or lions killed their sheep they'd be doomed. So he worked hard each day to perfect his aim.

Undoubtedly, the first time he held the sling and spun it, he felt awkward. It's safe to assume David's first stones missed their intended target. It's safe to assume this because that's how the story goes for everyone who tries something new for the first time. To win the battle that day, David had prepared with grit and faith for years in advance. And he eventually became the king of his domain.

GRIT AND FAITH

YOUR NEW DAILY HOMEWORK

You have your top twenty key relationships. You have your KR calendar ready to go. You know how you want to reach out to those people. Now it's time to start! And *just keep going.*

My challenge to you is to keep working on your key relationships calendar with a servant's heart to create the relationships that pay off in the end.

Digging for infinite referrals is hard work. It takes faith in the unknown and grit to get to the other side. *Don't give up until you do.* The last thing I want is for you to give up on the Infinite Referral Advantage® and have to live with the pain of never knowing just how close you were to creating the momentum that I've witnessed with Nick and so many of the other people I've helped. As long as you keep going, you're in the game. And the only way to truly fail is to quit altogether. Continue to learn from your perceived failures, make the necessary adjustments, and move forward.

My challenge to you is to keep working on your key relationships calendar with a servant's heart to create the relationships that pay off in the end. On those days when you feel defeated, I want you to think about the guy at the bottom of the cartoon. Consider what you would tell him, and use that advice for yourself!

The older I get, the more I can appreciate being present from one day to the next. And that is why I love to evaluate my progress twenty-four hours at a time. Don't get me wrong—I have a vision board and long-term goals that I'm working toward. But I only have certain moments in the year when I look at them. When people look at where I'm at now and ask me, "How did you do it?" my response is pretty simple: "One day at a time."

Doesn't that remind you of the old cliché that says, "After twenty-five years, she became an overnight success?"

"Slow and steady" isn't the sexiest answer, but I'm telling you, that's what works.

YOU'VE GOT THIS

I can honestly say that my favorite part of the Infinite Referral Advantage® is that it's *personal*. I've worked with thousands of people over the years, and each one executes their touchpoints and relationship building differently. I see it as one final advantage that you have over all the other Davids.

Don't you just love a little plot twist at the end? I sure do!

When you take what you've learned here and make it your own, staying consistent and true to who you are, it's incredibly powerful. No one can replicate your heart and the unique spin that you put into your relationships. Now go out there and make your world and the business you love a better place—one authentic connection at a time!

ACKNOWLEDGEMENTS

You are reading this book not because of me, but rather all of those who supported me throughout my life. If life truly is "a game" the score is kept based on the number of deep, rich, meaningful relationships we establish and maintain. Winners aren't determined by what they've amassed, true victory is earned by what they've shared. You are reading this book because so many have given so much of themselves to me. If you are one of those people, I am eternally grateful—and love you for it. As a token of my appreciation, I now pass along all that you've poured into me for the benefit of others.

ENDNOTES

Chapter One

1. Olson, Jeffrey G. *The Slight Edge: Turning Simple Disciplines into Massive Success.* Lake Dallas, TX: Success Books, 2013.

Chapter Two

1. Main, Kelly. "Small Business Statistics of 2024." Forbes, January 31, 2024. https://www.forbes.com/advisor/business/small-business-statistics/.

2. Keller, Gary, and Jay Papasan. *The One Thing: The Surprisingly Simple Truth Behind Extraordinary Results.* Austin, TX: Bard Press, 2021.

Chapter Four

1. Hyken, Shep. "Creating the WOW Experience." Forbes, June 27, 2021. https://www.forbes.com/sites/shephyken/2021/06/27/creating-the-wow-experience/?sh=71b18fe0ab60.

Chapter Eleven

1. William Butler Yeats Quotes. BrainyQuote.com, BrainyMedia Inc, 2024. https://www.brainyquote.com/quotes/william_butler_yeats_383082, accessed February 28, 2024.

2. Collins, Jim. *Good to Great: Why Some Companies Make the Leap … and Others Don't.* London: Random House, 2001.

Chapter Twelve

1. Sharma, Robin. "Robin Sharma Quote." AZQuotes.com. Accessed March 6, 2024. https://www.azquotes.com/quote/864603.

2. Gladwell, Malcolm. "The Unheard Story of David and Goliath." Malcolm Gladwell: The unheard story of David and Goliath | TED Talk, September 2013. https://www.ted.com/talks/malcolm_gladwell_the_unheard_story_of_david_and_goliath.

3. Dum. "PERSISTÊNCIA." DUM ILUSTRADOR, April 5, 2011. https://dumilustrador.blogspot.com/2011/. Used with permission.

ABOUT THE AUTHOR

Scott Grates is a leading authority in professional development, personal growth, mentorship, and relationship marketing. With an unwavering dedication to empowering small business owners, Scott's career centers on unlocking the transformative power of cultivating authentic relationships.

Having navigated the challenges of small business ownership for nearly two decades, Scott enjoys sharing insights gained from his personal journey from poverty in a small NY town to overseeing four businesses generating millions annually. Scott remains committed to serving underdogs by helping them tap into their potential and guiding them toward long-term success.

Beyond his professional endeavors, Scott immerses himself in family life, sports, church activities, and extensive travel adventures with his wife, Kelly and their three children, Tyler, Conner and Jenna. Their experiences are shared on the Love Living Local 315 podcast, where they put the Infinite Referral Advantage taught in Scott's Referrals Done Right book into action. By promoting fellow small businesses, schools, service groups and customers, Scott and Kelly connect with their community in meaningful ways.